Dedication

I want to dedicate this book to my father, Albert, who passed away on May 23, 2004, less than three weeks shy of his 91st birthday. If I can live my life as successfully and with as much nurturance as he did, dedicating every moment to his children and wife, if I can be half the father he was to me and my sister Gail, then I will truly be blessed.

Table of Contents

Preface &
Acknowledgments

Where do I come off presenting myself as an expert in raising children? After all, I have only done it once, and am not yet done. Some of you have raised many more children than I have (I am always daunted by my former secretary, Marian Jablonski, who raised ten children and all of them good kids—now adults). I guess you could say that I have the "credentials" for this. I am fairly bright, have earned a Ph.D. in developmental psychology, studied and taught child and adolescent development for 30 years, and am considered an expert in the moral and character development of children. But I think the real answer to the question is some mixture of "I don't know" and *chutzpah.* (*Chutzpah* is Yiddish for some sort of blend of gall, audacity, self-confidence, and an intrepid spirit.)

This whole expert-in-parenting thing actually began when I finished my Ph.D., and went to work for Larry Kohlberg at the Harvard Graduate School of Education. One day Carol Gilligan came into my office, and asked if I could bail her out by standing in for her to give a talk on discipline to parents at a local elementary school. With a touch of *chutzpah,* I agreed. I read up on research on the effects of reward and punishment on behavior, parenting styles, etc., and prepared a talk. It actually went quite well. Except for one moment, that is. I was extolling the virtues of rewards and cautioning about the potential perils of punishment when a man asked if I was saying never to use punishment. Being a good psychologist, I waffled. "Well, of course there are some times when punishment is recommended, such as when a child is about to put her hand on the stove or walk into traffic, and you can't wait to reward correct behavior. But generally, rewarding desirable behavior is much more effective than punishing undesirable behavior." I felt pretty good about that answer...until someone took me aside after the talk and informed me that the man who had asked the question was a known child abuser. I have never forgotten that, and for the ensuing 27 years, have felt guilty that I inadvertently provided him an "endorsement" for his cruelty. The field of parenting can indeed be a minefield.

So when I was approached to write a newspaper column on parenting for character, I had good reason to think twice about putting myself forward as an expert, and doing it so irrevocably, and in public. But in the quarter-century since that incident in the Boston elementary school, I felt that I had learned plenty, both from my professional work and from being a parent. At first, the newspaper column was supposed to be syndicated, as I was first asked to write this by a syndicator who thought there was a market for such a column. However, he was only able to attract one newspaper to sign on, the *Topeka Capitol-Journal.* Off I went, writing a column each week that appeared in the Sunday *TCJ.* As time went on and no other newspapers took the bait, three things happened: (1) I really began to enjoy writing the column; (2) I began sending it to many friends and colleagues who seemed to enjoy reading it; (3) the syndicator bailed out of the project. So I asked the *TCJ* if they wanted to continue working directly with me and not through the syndicator. We are now in our fourth year of our relationship, and I owe them a deep debt for taking the chance and sticking with me for all these years. They have given me an outlet for a voice that I have come to thoroughly enjoy, and I hope I have given them and their readers in Topeka some entertainment, information, and inspiration.

I also want to thank my good friend and colleague, Phil Vincent, for conceiving this book and supporting its production, along with his colleagues at Character Development Group, especially Dixon Smith, Stacy Shelp-Peck, Andrea Grenadier, and Ellen Bradley. This book would never have existed without their imagination, support, and expertise.

But the biggest thanks go to all the "mothers" and "fathers" in my life who taught me in the trenches of real-life experience what good parenting truly is. As I look back over the more than a half century that stands as my life, I have come to recognize how many people helped raise me and modeled good parenting. I could never mention them all, and I humbly and sincerely acknowledge all of those I couldn't possibly list here.

There are all the "mothers" of my two childhood neighborhoods, who were the village that raised this child (Heather Wasserman in Kew Gardens; Phyllis Rosenberg, Sandy Elkins, and Blossom Rappaport in North Woodmere). And the dads who coached my Little League teams and played catch with me. There were all my aunts and uncles and my (mostly older, female) cousins who were a secure and comforting safety net, who loved me unconditionally and looked out for me. And my unofficial aunts and uncles, my parents' very extensive friendship network (like Sylvia and Jerry Thomases and Renee and Ephram Krangel). There were my school teachers like Mr. Sloan, my sixth-grade teacher, a burly formidable U.S. Marine WWII veteran—really a thinly disguised teddy bear who made school fun and remarkably safe for a group of sixth graders situated in an all seventh- and eighth-grade building. And like Mrs. Phillips, my high school Spanish teacher, who set remarkably high standards and demanded and provided respect for all of us (and got me, not a natural language learner, to be fluent by the time I graduated). There are the Jesuit Fathers (like Frs. Gene Merz, John Naus, and Victor Adangba) for and with whom I worked for 20 years at Marquette University, and who demonstrated supererogation in their calling to care for all the creatures of the world. And my professional mentors, most notably Larry Kohlberg and Tony Kuchan, who, academically and personally, taught me so much about how to care for others. And my colleague and dear friend, Clark Power, who exudes a unique blend of wisdom, intelligence, and love.

When I am asked how and why I have come to study character development, I can only think of one answer: my parents. I was so fortunate to be raised in a family and community that was anchored in love and a steadfast commitment to moral values. I often think of the unlikely parallel between my upbringing and that of my good friend Clifton Taulbert. Cliff was raised in a homogenously economically deprived African-American community in the rural, segregated Mississippi delta. I was raised in a reasonably affluent, homogenously Jewish-American community in the suburbs of New York City. Almost different planets. All of Cliff's writings are steeped in the positive values of his upbringing, the sense of community and character that formed the Petrie dish of his personal growth. That seems so true for me as well. And my parents, Phyllis and Albert Berkowitz, were the conduits for that socialization in classic Jewish values like charity and justice and American values like work ethic and freedom. I never had a reason to doubt their love nor their willingness to sacrifice for me and my sister. That sense of being cherished and protected is so much of who I am. Yet they set high standards, both for achievement and for morality, that were utterly clear. I literally would not be here if not for them, and would never have been who I am without them either.

Finally, I have learned most about how to parent over the past two decades from my wife, Judy, and my son, Danny. When I began teaching child and adolescent development, I was in my mid 20s, newly married, and not yet near being a parent. I felt like an impostor, a charlatan, telling my students about how children develop, and particularly about how to raise them well. And then my son was born. Not only did I now have my parental certificate of authenticity, but I finally began to learn the truth about child development and parenting. I remember my graduate school professor, Carolyn Shantz, a leading expert in child psychology, telling me as a naïve 22-year-old, that once you have children, all the book learning goes out the window. My son has been my greatest teacher about parenting. He humbles me daily as I see the complexity of doing it right, as I stumble and bumble through the Escher-esque landscape of parenting. He challenges me directly and indirectly as I try to figure out how to do this parenting thing right. And, as you read the columns in this book, he becomes the protagonist and provides me endless material for writing about parenting, just as he has done for decades in my lectures to my students—all of whom feel like they know him personally by now. My wife is a remarkable mother. A natural. Her intuition, intelligence, and flair for parenting never cease to impress me. I cannot imagine what a mess I would have made of raising Danny, if not for her. I have learned so much from her about how to care, how to maintain perspective, how to craft messages, how to show unconditional love. I may have the Ph.D. in child development, but she is the true expert in our family.

So, after all, I have been blessed with so many models of and teachers about parenting that perhaps it was not a matter of *chutzpah* to present myself as an expert, because it is not me out there alone writing these columns—it is all of them guiding my hands as I type these words.

Marvin Berkowitz
St. Louis, Missouri
October 6, 2004

Foreword

PETER YARROW

Marvin W. Berkowitz is a trailblazer whose path will surely be followed by others; if so, our children will be very fortunate. He is the only person in America to occupy an endowed chair in character education, his being at the University of Missouri–St. Louis.

Marvin's unique position and breadth of experience, which straddles the academic, the grass roots, and the journalistic arenas, provides him a special platform from which to advance his work and that of his colleagues, all of whom are dedicated to the emotional, physical, and psychological well-being of children.

Transcending the enthusiasms for the latest pedagogical fad, Marvin helps separate the wheat from the chaff of new efforts in the field of character education and civic engagement. With the broadest and most holistic cutting edge views of ongoing progress in his and other related fields, Marvin is deeply respected for his advice, guidance, and wisdom, which he offers warmly and passionately to the entire field of child development and educational reform, as it seeks new pathways toward the education of the whole child: the academic, as well as the emotional, social, and moral sides of their growth, i.e., the development of their character.

His no nonsense "show me the data" perspective is coupled with an open and adventurously idealistic heart. Marvin helps to define, and energize, the most productive routes for children to succeed, with primary attention focused on "the other side of the report card."

Why is this book, and Marvin's work, so crucially important?

Simply stated, and characterized with the passion that it deserves, I believe that the future health and stability of the world may well depend upon Marvin's work, and the work of others like him; it may well rest upon our determination to adopt his advocacies as part of our own life's work—as activists, educators, parents, and concerned, contributory, members of society. Though it may sound calamitous to some, and for others these words will resonate as a wake-up call, I believe that such work might be decisive in determining, not only the future well-being of our world, but our very survival.

This perspective has become very important to me and my own work in preventing youth violence and promoting social-emotional learning and character development. I came to this way of thinking by a route I'd like to share with you, starting with some basic assumptions followed by my steps in thinking this through and reaching these conclusions.

ASSUMPTIONS AND STEPS

Children need to grow up to respect themselves and others for more important reasons than the stylishness of their sneakers.

We generally accept the fact that our children need to grow up to value and respect themselves and other children for their intrinsic goodness, kindness, and caring shown to one another. If not, they will more likely grow up to be not only intolerant and unappreciative of people different from themselves, they will, in large part, emulate far too large a segment of our adult society. They will basically trade healthy self-regard for the ultimately unsatisfying pursuit of fame, power, and money. Those who follow this route will, I believe, miss the basics of what life is all about. Sadly, these children will simply be emulating adult role models, some of them famous, that they watch on reality TV and other shows and movies. Also, in too many cases they will be emulating and recapitulating the behavior of their own parents.

Elementary school students, well on their way to engaging in such vacuous competition for power, money, and fame are learning to measure their own and others' worth by the grandness of their parents' houses, the cost of their parents' cars, the right sneakers, and the right gold chains.

Without an intervention, such children will grow up to escalate the problems we face in the world.

If children do not value themselves and others principally because of the amount of effort and heart they devote to caring for one another then, I believe, they will inevitably accelerate the current downward spiral of spirit and heart of our society—our humanity as a people. Our generosity, in mind and deed, toward the least fortunate among us, will continue to decline, as will our societal health and happiness. Such a change will ultimately endanger the safety of the world, as it already has in so many ways.

If competition for privilege rules, freedoms will have to diminish as we move closer to fulfilling the Orwellian prophecy.

As powerfully explained by Robert Wright in a *New York Times* op-ed article, if the above kind of soulless competition continues unchecked, then inequality of circumstance will increase as people, within and between nations, become more deeply divided into the haves and the have-nots. The privileged will increasingly have to protect themselves against intensified anger and resentment fueled by such inequality. Protection of the haves will necessitate the abbreviation of rights such as privacy and legal process and will result in the setting of elitist public policy. This, of course, is already happening.

With modern-day technology, unlike in years past, vast inequities are apparent to haves and have-nots alike. Advances in communication, through CNN, the web, etc. have opened a Pandora's box. Those who wish to oppose such inequity can do so by using the tools of today's technology to great advantage, in ways that were previously unheard of. They can do so nationally and internationally. Some will do so constructively, through education and programs that move us toward a world of greater fairness, but others will do so through the tools of terrorism, by mobilizing the resentment and hatred born of such inequity. In such a circumstance, without addressing this crucial dilemma, terrorism and war will increasingly become a more precipitous threat.

The elimination of rights of all to protect this inequity and address this danger of terrorism will endanger life in a democracy, as we have known it.

Democracy itself is at stake as well as, perhaps, our last chance for peace.

If such inequity persists unchecked, the foundations of democracy, which rely upon the existence of the freedom of expression, including opposition to governmental policies and opposition to war that is ill-considered or unnecessary, will be threatened. In a worst-case scenario, democracy as a system of government will no longer be viable, and life as we know it in the so-called free world will change dramatically. We have already begun to see such changes, changes that must be identified, evaluated, and stopped, for reasons of our very survival.

THE CONCLUSION: OUR CHILDREN ARE THE KEY; READ THIS BOOK

The preservation of democracy, and much else that we hold dear, may well rely on the way we bring up our children. Either they are educated to recapitulate our society's deep dilemmas, and repeat the mistakes that got us into this frightening downward slide, or they will get in touch with their hearts, souls, and ideals, and re-ignite our respect for one another—start us on a new path. (Actually only partially new. We were once much more like what we now erroneously believe ourselves to be.)

Children could continue to embrace a perspective held by far too many adults. They could, as do many adults, grow up to accept disrespect, emotional violence, and bullying as a fact of life, and regard it as simply a natural rite of passage among children. They could grow up to consider emotional violence broadcast on reality TV as entertaining. They could grow up with battered psyches, crippled by such tacitly approved socio-pathological behavior.

PRODUCING A DIFFERENT RESULT

To produce a different result, we must make sure our children are treated with, and treat each other with, respect for many more reasons than we might have previously thought were important. Children must not be subjected to painful ridicule, name-calling, intolerance, and bullying, lest they be condemned to recapitulate this brutality and visit it upon the next generation. Such behavior is the base of what is called, by the Anti-Defamation League, the "triangle of hate." What seems somewhat innocent behavior in children evolves into bigotry, intolerance, racism, hatred, war, and even genocide. We must stop it before it starts because the more evolved such attitudes are, the harder they become to counter. In fact, we typically feel that we cannot turn around such attitudes and perceptions that feed hatred, suspicion, and intolerance in adults. Once they are imbedded, it's difficult, perhaps impossible, to change them.

We urgently need to assure the development of the habits of respect in children, and provide role models among those who shepherd their development, so that they can grow up to be caring, kind, participating members of society. Addressing the developmental needs of our children is virtually the task of saving democracy and, probably, reaching for our last chance for pervasive, enduring peace.

Having shared my assumptions about the critical necessity of promoting the positive, pro-social development of youth, I want to now explain how I have arrived at this perspective.

HOW I HAVE COME TO ADOPT THIS PERSPECTIVE

I have spent the major portion of my adult life dedicated to trying to eliminate inequity, mostly through the vehicle of music. Music, particularly folk music, can help people share their hopes and dreams, validate each other's convictions, and empower them to act on such shared passions and perspectives. In short, such music can create community.

Along with many others with a similar intention, I have lived the reality of a mutual validation and empowerment process, utilizing music as a tool, during the Civil Rights movement, the peace movement, many other movements that followed, and most recently the movement to assure children a safe, non-bullying, ridicule-free environment in which to grow and learn. Together, we have sought to help find heart-connecting threads that energize efforts for seeking greater justice and fairness in society.

Unfortunately, however, I have recently come to the conclusion that, although many of our efforts have resulted in meaningful gains in policy change, attitudes and behavior, changing the hearts of adults is another matter entirely. Lasting change emanating from such efforts has been incrementally successful—meaningful, but for our own time and the scope of our dilemmas, not nearly rapid enough.

To look at past efforts of the movements is to observe serious "two steps forward and one step backward" motion. Our efforts to eliminate the biases and animosities and historical hatred that lead to bloodshed and war have been only marginally successful.

We must do more than that now, and we must do it so much more quickly than in previous years. The lessons of 9/11 and ensuing events took us quickly on a course that ratchets up the urgency for change of the heart of society, not just its laws and policies.

I believe that such change cannot be done with advocacies among adults alone. For better, and more frequently for worse, adults are pretty much attached to their conceptions—and misconceptions. They tend to irrationally and doggedly defend their perspectives. We become, psychologically and sociologically, what we have habitually "eaten" and can insist on staying that way, frequently because of fear, self-esteem, and the need to preserve our personal and psychological investment in our formative process.

It is only through children, and adults' partnerships with them, initiated by teachers, parents, and others, that we can help to shape the development of children before they become committed to the ways of prejudice, selfishness, and hatred. We can open young hearts so that they will not perpetuate past animosities and retributive equations. However, we must move quickly and decisively to save the next generation, our future, and ourselves before an unstoppable momentum carries society beyond the point of no return.

I absolutely believe that if we are to heal what is wrong in the world before it implodes or explodes, or degenerates into Orwellian-style gated communities, we must direct our priority efforts to making changes through and with our children, starting the day they are born, way before they are "taught to hate and fear." We must make sure that such efforts are sustained, so that these changes will no longer be susceptible to reversal. Only then will we end the cycle of societal pathology that threatens us.

In short, the heart and spirit of society must be changed and recreated for the next generation. Nothing short of that, I believe, can turn us away from a most dangerous, and potentially terminally destructive path, toward which we are now headed pell-mell.

To me, the task is to interrupt the cycle of illness, be it medical, biological, psychosocial, addictive, criminal, child or family abusing, etc. The only way to do that, in terms of what I consider to be potentially terminal illness in our society, is to work with children, among children, in conjunction with children, and intervene before the previous generation infects the next generation with its diseases.

The answer to our dilemmas is intuitively understood by virtually everyone who has chosen education as a profession. Educators certainly do not become educators because they want to become rich. They do so because they feel that one's life purpose can be realized by offering children a window of opportunity to grow up to be whole, healthy people, to celebrate their gifts and capacities. They hope to rejoice in children using such gifts to devote themselves to the betterment of humankind.

If there is one group of people in society whose very lives have been dedicated from the start to doing exactly what we need to do to reset our course, it is educators.

We must look to them, to the children themselves, and to parents. Parents may be carrying the inherited diseases of singular devotion to fame, power, and money, and may be steeped in prejudice and intolerance, but they love their children, and I believe that it is for this reason that the best way for us to affect the adult population is actually through children themselves.

If children can teach their parents to use safety belts and to stop smoking, perhaps children can also teach their parents the rudiments of civility, of acceptance of "the other," of generosity, of grace, respect, and caring.

I have come to view my own previous efforts, if they are to be repeated with the expectation of success in today's world, to be inadequate to the task. The methodologies of change for the future must emerge strongly and quickly, so far have we fallen from what was once a kind of inherent goodness, belief in ourselves, and a kind of naive, but wonderful societal grace. If we embrace past efforts and methodologies as the sole tools of change in the future, our efforts will, I believe, be doomed to failure.

Such activism of the kind that has engaged me for over four decades is inadequate for the creation of lasting change of heart that is needed in these times. The timeline for the kind of change that we need right now, and upon which peace and the survival of the planet depends, is far too urgent and its opponents far too powerful, to believe that we do not need to adopt a new frame of reference to address this imperative.

I believe that the new basis for our efforts must trust that if goodness becomes the staple of our children's education, that they will naturally gravitate toward humane solutions to society's ills and dilemmas. Happily, I believe that such a premise, even if not adopted by some, will not be opposed by anyone. How can anyone want to oppose a movement that seeks to instill goodness and fairness as a basic construct of children's lives?

The beauty of the premise is that the enemy of this kind of change does not recognize itself. It believes that it does embody fairness and goodness already, and that privilege and inequity, as it exists today, is indeed fair and good. They do not realize that if children are given the tools of respectful and compassionate exchange, learn to value themselves and others for their goodness, service to, and expressed love of one another and society, learn to resolve conflict, on a reflexive basis, peacefully, these children will be far less likely to embrace the inequities of yesterday.

They will be far less likely to perpetuate the inequities that fan hatred and lead to the waging of war as a ready solution to international conflict, or as anything other than a last, last, last possible resort. They will not embrace the concept that might makes right. They will intuitively move toward the kind of a world in which it is commonly accepted that greater freedom for all leads to peace; that sharing of the wealth and the preservation of the earth leads to survival; that goodness and fairness need to be invoked as a first and hopefully last strategy; and that our lives will be happier and safer if we do so.

SOME FINAL WORDS

I send you this message so that you will perhaps examine the work of Marvin Berkowitz with these thoughts in mind as you read his book.

The truth is that we can all do something to help make the change that is needed. The most important ingredient for change is the will to make it happen.

I believe that Marvin's book presents us with an opportunity and a tool. If we use it wisely, and embrace it fully, it could become a handbook for the survival of everything we value in our society and of our society itself.

> Peter Yarrow
> February 15, 2004

Anger
and Conflict

The Art of Anger

THINK OF ALL THE WORDS WE HAVE FOR BEING ANGRY: ticked off, furious, enraged, annoyed, miffed, irked, rankled, and others. We sure have lots of ways to say we are angry.

But anger has gotten somewhat of a bad rap in our culture. When we think of anger, we think of being out of control, a loose cannon. We think of the need for anger management. We think of being immature or needing counseling. And in many cases those are all fair assessments.

But anger is real, it is legitimate, it is authentic. And it is inevitable, at least for most folks. Some of you out there simply do not get angry. I once had a secretary like that, and it completely mystified me. I simply couldn't understand it. Mind you, I was impressed and valued her ability to take in stride life's slings and arrows. There is even research to say that such an ability relates to longevity.

But for most people, anger will be part of their emotional repertoire and life's experiences. So there are two basic questions. When is anger appropriate? And what do you *do* with your anger?

In this case, I am most interested in expressing anger to children, and how that affects their development of character. It is important to note that for infants, it is never appropriate to let them feel your emotional wrath. They cannot understand it but will negatively feel it. They don't know what it means or why it is there; they are just frightened and disrupted by it.

But as children get older, they can learn that parental anger is an indicator that something has really upset mom or dad. However, it is important that the anger never threaten the child's well-being. It should not become a physical or psychological threat. It should, instead, be an expression of mom or dad's emotional state rather than an assault on the child.

It should be explained clearly. Young children, especially pre-schoolers, tend to think that bad events are their fault. So if mom or dad is very angry, they may assume that they are the cause of the anger, even when that is far from accurate.

Parental anger can serve to teach children what is important to parents. Or what is dangerous or prohibited. And it can teach about emotions and emotion management, something children are not born with, but need to develop.

In his book *Take Back Your Kids*, William Doherty has an entire chapter called "Why anger-free parenting does not work." I recall visiting Eugene, Oregon once and witnessing such parental ineptitude.

Now if you haven't been to Eugene, it is a living time capsule. Eugene is where old hippies go, not to die but to raise new generations of hippies. Before you old hippies and ex-hippies out there get offended, please know that I am one of you. I went to college in the late 1960s and early 1970s, and I can march for peace and tie-dye with the best of them.

I was wandering through Eugene's weekend open air market, looking at candle stands and incense booths, when I noticed a young mother and her young son, who was about three years old. The child was crying hysterically. The mother was trying to calm the child down. In a very calm voice, she kept repeating "I would really like it better if you stopped crying." Over and over and over. It was futile and useless, and had absolutely no impact on the hysterical child in her arms.

I am not trying to suggest that anger should be the first line of defense in such a case. In fact, distraction is a much more effective strategy.

But sometimes, showing your emotions, even strong or negative emotions, is acceptable parenting. Kids will experience those same emotions and they need to know that they are okay, that others feel them as well, and that there are appropriate and inappropriate ways of manifesting and managing them.

Inevitable Conflict

WE DON'T LIKE TO ADMIT THAT WE HAVE ARGUMENTS, especially with our families. Marital spats, kids' tantrums, and noisy arguments between parents and kids are often not spoken about with others. Or even between the combatants. But it is important to recognize that conflict is inevitable. In fact, when I meet a couple or a family that claims to never argue, I worry about whether they are truly communicating.

Now, don't get me wrong. I am not an advocate for conflict, fighting, arguing, and so on. I am just a realist. It is going to happen, even to the best of us.

The real issue with kids is not whether or not there will be conflict, but how we deal with it when it happens—and it will. Do we pretend it isn't there? Do we make matters worse by playing

> **When I meet a couple or a family that claims to never argue, I worry about whether they are truly communicating.**

"gotcha last!"? Or do we find a constructive way to resolve the conflict and actually grow and move forward from it?

Recently, I was offering a workshop to child care workers and educators. One of them told me of a case where one of the adolescent girls with whom she works had a huge fight with her mother. Mom came into the room and found the girl watching something on TV that mom thought was inappropriate for her. This is not an uncommon nor an earth-shattering issue. But it warrants mom's intervention. Unfortunately, this mother apparently did not know how to effectively deal with conflicts. The daughter resisted her mother's (probably very mean and attacking) request to turn off the TV show. It degenerated into a power struggle and ultimately, into a physical fight over the TV remote control. And it became severe enough that child care professionals had to get involved.

I remember years ago reading an article by the late Fred Rogers, one of the most truly wise and gifted people when it comes to all things children. He said that it is important for parents to monitor what their children watch. But rather than suggesting a prison guard control approach, he suggested watching questionable material with your child and talking to them about it. This seems a far more reasonable response than escalation into a physical fight over a remote control for the TV. The fight evolved into something else beyond a disagreement over what is appropriate viewing, and into a lack of effective communication skills and ultimately a breakdown in the parent and child relationship.

All families should learn conflict resolution strategies, and parents need to learn what we try to teach preschoolers...use your words and not your hands. But use your words effectively to reduce conflict and to promote the development of your child's character.

Parental Conflict and Kids' Character

IT IS NOW A WELL-KNOWN FINDING IN PSYCHOLOGY THAT parental conflict is potentially harmful for a child's development. This includes emotional harm, such as depression; behavioral problems, including delinquency; social deficits, such as poor peer relations; and academic problems.

It is also clear and inevitable that all children will witness parental conflict. But some occurrences of parental conflict are harmful and others are not. Fortunately, researchers are beginning to understand some of the ways in which parental conflict is or isn't damaging to kids' character and general development.

> **Families must strive to be a consistently supportive unit, for kids need to feel and know that the family is stable and committed to itself and all its members.**

One set of studies by Patrick Davies and his colleagues (published by the Society for Research in Child Development) sheds much light on this issue. In one of their studies, they looked at some of the features of parenting, families, and parental conflict that can buffer the negative effects of witnessing inevitable conflict.

They identify three broad areas: 1) family cohesion; 2) interparental relationship satisfaction; and 3) interparental emotional expressiveness. In their own words, "interparental conflict is hypothesized to take on a different, more benign meaning in the context of warm, cohesive, and expressive family relationships."

The idea is that interparental conflict in such a family is less likely to be understood as threatening by kids. If families truly and consistently care about each other and express their emotions in both positive and negative situations, then such a spat will not be seen as threatening to the family or to the child.

Therefore, families must strive to be a consistently supportive unit, for kids need to feel and know that the family is stable and committed to itself and all its members. As a result, witnessing parents in conflict will not likely make kids emotionally insecure, thereby contributing to other negative behavioral and developmental outcomes.

Kids need to see, feel, and truly believe that their parents really do care about each other. If they know that, then a momentary conflict will not be seen as a threat to the marriage or to the family. So let your kids know that you love and are committed to each other by expressing your emotions openly and honestly. Let your joy and anger out. Let your disappointment and elation show, and let your fears and satisfactions be apparent. If kids routinely witness your good and bad feelings, then they will not be so threatened by observing your interparental conflict.

Conflict is not bad in and of itself. If it occurs in a context of a cohesive, expressive family, then it is unlikely to do other than teach kids about the variability of life, as well as the elasticity and resilience of relationships. But if kids don't know the family is secure and are unused to witnessing your emotions, then they may suffer scars from your inevitable parental conflicts.

For the sake of building your kids' character, let them in on your emotions and on the strengths and stability of your relationships within the family.

Character
and Society

Welcome to the Experiment

I HAVE NEWS FOR YOU. YOU ARE PART OF AN EXPERIMENT. No, this is not one of those secret experiments where some government agency puts drugs in your Yoo-Hoo without you knowing about it. But you are in an experiment, nonetheless.

In fact, so are all of your neighbors. And relatives. And me. All Americans are part of a great experiment. In fact, America is an experiment—an experiment in democracy.

When our forefathers (Thomas Jefferson, James Madison, George Washington, John Adams, Benjamin Franklin, etc.) first formed the U.S., they were taking a big chance in designing a new type of country. We tend to forget this now, because it has been around for so long. But when it started, it was very daring and new, this democracy. How do you get citizens to actually run a country, of the people, by the people, and for the people?

This is a column about parenting and children's character, so you are probably wondering why I am talking about history and government. When our forefathers were designing this

> When our forefathers were designing this great experiment in democracy, they realized that if it was going to succeed, it needed a certain kind of citizen... ones who were honest, who were dedicated to the ideals of democracy, who cared about community and the welfare of their fellow citizens, who were courageous....

great experiment in democracy, they realized that if it was going to succeed, it needed a certain kind of citizen. It needed citizens who were honest, who were dedicated to the ideals of democracy, who cared about community and the welfare of their fellow citizens, who were courageous, and so on. They realized that, for the great experiment to work, we needed citizens with good character. Where do we get such citizens? Well, we grow them. Each generation is charged with insuring that their children grow up with good character, or else the experiment will fail.

This experiment did not end in the 1700s, or the 1800s, or even the 1900s. And now that the 2000s are here, it continues. Every generation can be the last. If we continue to raise selfish children, eventually the country will crumble. Because a true democracy cannot survive made of citizens with weak or selfish character. It demands a citizenry with good character because a democratic nation *is* its citizens.

What exactly is democratic character? It is being responsible and caring, and rests heavily on respecting others simply because they are people. It is being committed to the common good, participating in society, and being critical and thoughtful about important issues. It is being literate, being a good listener, being cooperative, and being confident.

So how can you help to raise a child to have democratic character? The same way that you affect other parts of their character. You model it (if you don't vote, neither will they). You talk to them about it (if you don't care about politics, neither will they). You reward it (if they know you are proud of them for helping the local community, they will be more likely to continue to do so). You care about them, love them, talk seriously with them. You respect them and their ideas, and you encourage them to participate in their family, their communities, and their nation.

This also can be done in schools and communities. For instance, the Citizenship Education Clearing House (CECH) in St. Louis (314-516-6820) helps kids get involved in being good citizens by getting them to engage in the voting process. And the Center for

Civic Education (www.civiced.org) in California puts out lots of valuable information on educating kids to be democratic citizens. You could even join their "National Campaign to Promote Civic Education."

So when you think about how you raise your children, please understand just how much is at stake. If your child's future is not enough to motivate you to parent well for character, then how about the fate of the country? Didn't realize how important you were, did you? Well, citizen, now you know.

Tolerance

WE HEAR A LOT OF TALK ABOUT PROMOTING TOLERANCE these days. Tolerance of different racial groups in America, tolerance of religious groups in Northern Ireland and the Middle East, tolerance of ethnic groups in the Balkans, and so on.

Curricula are being adopted by our nation's schools in an attempt to promote tolerance and its understanding. Organizations concerned with tolerance are springing up like daisies. My personal favorite is a project of the Southern Poverty Law Center (www.splcenter.org) and its web project called tolerance.org (www.tolerance.org), which combats racism, hatred, and prejudice. There is even a journal called *Teaching Tolerance.*

But I have never forgotten a Sunday School lesson that touched on the subject of tolerance about 40 years ago. I was shocked that day when the teacher said, "'Tolerate' is one of the dirtiest words in the English language!" What he said seemingly went against everything my parents had taught me. It took some time for me to figure out what he actually meant.

The word tolerance has two meanings. One has to do with accepting differences, and this is the concept that educational institutions are working hard to teach our children. It's important that they learn to both accept and tolerate people who are in some ways unlike themselves, such as people who dress, worship, speak, or act differently. This kind of tolerance is good, because it's an expression of a moral principle upon which our nation was founded: the belief that all people are created equal and should be treated that way. Put another way, it means that all people deserve respect simply because they are people. Indeed, respect for individuals is central to most religious and moral theories.

So what about my Sunday School teacher's seeming condemnation of tolerance? Was he misguided? Weird? Simply wrong? Not at all. You'll remember my mentioning that there was another meaning of the word tolerance. That meaning has to do with allowing something to happen that you believe to be offensive, wrong, or harmful. That kind of tolerance is bad.

So how do we resolve the seeming contradiction between an argument for tolerance and an argument against it? We must explain to our children that there are some things that must always be tolerated and others that must never be. And we must teach them that from time to time, they will find it necessary to take a stand on such issues. Because many others won't.

Simply put, we must teach our children to tolerate differences, such as not persecuting others because of a difference of skin color or because they were born to a culture with other dietary laws or language. At the same time, we must also teach our children that they should never tolerate someone who oppresses or discriminates against others, violates the rights of others, or violates basic moral principles.

My column is about parenting for character, so you're probably wondering where all this is heading. Well, where do you think children learn about tolerance? They learn it from their parents. And where do our children learn to accept non-moral differences and also learn to take a stand against moral transgressions? They learn that from their parents, too. So parents have to pay strict attention to their positions regarding what should and shouldn't be tolerated. It's important that we accept others who look or act differently. But it's of equal importance that we take a stand against moral transgressions, such as fighting against racism, sexism, and ageism.

That's what we want to teach our children.

All Worked Up

W.R. of California writes: "My husband and I disagree about a parenting issue. He wants our fourteen-year-old son to do volunteer work in the community, but I think he is too young and that his time could be better spent on his schoolwork. What do you think?"

WORK IS AN IMPORTANT PART OF A TEEN'S PREPARATION for becoming an adult. Teens need to apprentice at work so that they may learn how to become productive members of society. However, work comes in many different forms.

When we think of "work,"we might think of the Seven Dwarves shouldering picks and shovels as they head off to heavy labor. And when we think of teens and work, we might think of a local kid tossing newspapers from her bicycle, working in a fast-food establishment, or worse, an abusive child labor sweatshop. However, work is not limited to what brings in a paycheck. Work also includes activities such as schoolwork, volunteer work, and yes, even family chores.

So both W.R. and her husband are correct. I believe that kids need to spend time not only on schoolwork, but also doing volunteer work, which teaches the value of contributing to the community in which they live. Each activity, in its own way, helps them to learn and grow. Plus, both types of work teach responsibility, self-discipline, and perseverance. Kids who learn to work hard to succeed in school are developing skills that will help them throughout the rest of their lives. And kids who learn to work hard to benefit others are developing characteristics that will help them to become caring, compassionate, contributing members of society.

In fact, many schools from elementary to college are initiating programs that require community service (sometimes called service learning) as a graduation requirement. That's because work not only helps students learn, it also helps to build character.

But there can also be too much of a good thing (with the possible exception of chocolate truffles, Van Morrison CDs, and the NCAA Final Four games). Research shows us that high school students who work more than twenty hours per week become less involved in school, engage in more delinquent behaviors (including drug use and fighting), get less exercise and sleep, skip breakfast more frequently, receive lower grades, and fight more with their parents.

And, unfortunately, that same research shows that even if the students later cut back on work hours, most of those behaviors do not improve. Sadly, the damage lingers.

> **Kids who learn to work hard to benefit others are developing characteristics that will help them to become caring, compassionate, contributing members of society.**

Kids need a balanced life if they are going to get a fair shake at becoming good people. They need rest and sleep. They need time to daydream. They need fun and play. They need exercise. They need to learn. They need to work. And of course, they need love and support.

One more thing: From the question above, I notice that W.R. and her husband can't agree on what is best for their son. Family specialists are in consensus that it is best if parents can speak with a united voice. Realistically speaking, however, that is not always possible.

One might ask, "If the parents can't come to an informed agreement, then how can they expect to establish unified policies for their child?" The answer: Initiate honest and respectful family discussion. You'll find that, surprisingly often, a suitable resolution will emerge of its own accord.

In summary, it is a good idea for kids to do volunteer work *and* to do schoolwork. But we must be careful not to merge two good ideas into a single bad one. Just remember that when it comes to developing character..."work works."

Value Added

AS LONG AS PEOPLE HAVE BEEN RUNNING AROUND THIS planet, some have wondered why we are here. What is the point to all of this? And is there a right way to live? For more than two thousand years, philosophers have struggled with this question, so don't expect me to answer it here. But I will take a stab at offering some advice for parents that has to do with justifying taking up space on this increasingly crowded planet.

In their book *High Risk: Children Without Conscience*, Ken Magid and Carole McKelvey argue that kids who are abused and neglected become "trust bandits." By this, they mean that such damaging parenting produces kids who prey on humanity. Kids without conscience, kids who don't care about others and have no qualms about hurting and taking from other people.

I have argued before that parents need to teach children to understand, care about, and adhere to positive values. If parents want children to develop good character, they need to focus on such values. One such value is to leave the world a better place than when you entered it—to make a positive contribution to the world. Elaine Blechman, a psychologist at the University of Colorado who designs child and family therapy programs for at-risk kids, considers this rule to be one of the solutions to child misbehavior. She recommends that families emphasize that and other healthy values, and offers ways to successfully achieve this.

Think about it. If everyone improved the world even a little bit during their lifetimes, then the state of the world would gradually improve. Less crime, less suffering, less hatred, less selfishness. That is a pretty attractive proposition.

This is a clear contradiction to the common refrain, "I am only one person. What possible difference can one person make?" You may have heard the old story about the little boy who stood on a beach covered with stranded starfish. He slowly picked them up one at a time and tossed them back into the ocean. A man approached and said, "You know, you're wasting your time. There must be thousands of starfish on this beach, and you can only throw back a few. What possible difference can you make?" The child thoughtfully looked at the starfish in his hand, and answered, "It makes a difference to this one."

Parenting for character not only helps the child live a happier, more fulfilling life, but also contributes to the whole world—one starfish at a time.

Communicating

Family Meetings

I HAVE WRITTEN ABOUT THE IMPORTANCE OF GIVING KIDS a voice in family decisions. It has to do with maintaining open communication lines within the family. And one excellent way to do this is through family meetings.

In his book *Raising Good Children*, Thomas Lickona talks about a unique approach to family meetings. He describes a ten-step "fairness approach to conflict," whereby, initially, family members work to understand each other's point of view. Next, they try to solve the problems at hand. And lastly, the group members review the solution to make sure it is working.

I first introduced the concept to my graduate students a few years ago. The following week a student returned having employed the technique with her two elementary school-age sons. "It worked like a charm," she said enthusiastically. "Usually, my sons fight all day long. So I called a family meeting to discuss the problem and the boys haven't had a fight in the last five days. It's nothing less than a miracle." Apparently, they heard one another's points of view, perhaps for the first time, and agreed on methods to constructively approach and solve their conflicts. Better yet, because they felt they "owned" the solution, they willingly adhered to it without further complaint.

I teach educators how to employ a similar technique for solving classroom and school problems. "Class meetings" are advocated by many of the leading programs in character education, such as in the invaluable book, *Ways We Want Our Class To Be*, by the Developmental Studies Center (www.devstu.org). On the site, you'll find many resources designed to help build relationships and resolve conflicts.

Class meetings and family meetings should not be used exclusively for problem solving. Such meetings can also be useful for evaluating progress, for sharing, for planning, or just discussing ideas and issues. For instance, hold a family meeting to discuss your kids' thoughts and concerns about terrorism and their perceived vulnerabilities. After all, they are thinking about it anyway, so it's better for them to share their thoughts with caring adults than to hold inside those feelings of fear, uncertainty, and apprehension.

You will know once and for all that such meetings are a part of your family's culture when your kids begin taking the initiative to request a family meeting. (This holds true for schools as well.) Rather than perceiving such actions as being indicative of family problems, parents and educators should instead should see them as a sign that the kids care enough to deal head-on with their concerns. And that's a great way to prepare for dealing with the many curve balls life will throw at them when they become adults.

Just this week, my son called for a family meeting. He felt that recently I had been a bit of a grouch and was incessantly snapping at him. Indeed, we were both a bit grumpy and the situation had reached the point where we had been avoiding one another. Our family meeting enabled my son and me to clear the air, and we have been getting along great ever since. Without the meeting, we probably would have continued on a downward spiral, so I was actually glad that he requested the meeting. It took some guts on his part—but that in itself is a solid component of character. So it was a win/win situation.

Talking Values

PEOPLE EVENTUALLY CHOOSE THEIR FRIENDS, THEIR mates, their heroes, etc. based at least in part on the similarity of their values. For instance, when dating we usually start with physical attraction, but for a relationship to endure, it eventually requires that we find compatibility between our values. Do you both think people should speak their minds or is privacy and tact more important? Is having nice things at the top of your list of personal achievements, or sacrificing for those less fortunate than you? Is showing one's feelings desirable? Do you like public recognition or do you get embarrassed when a fuss is made about you? And so on.

It is important to recognize that we all hold many values and they are of very different sorts, so we will not likely find another person who has the precise set of values that we do. But we often wish we could, and sometimes fool ourselves into thinking that we have.

One psychologist argued that marriages begin with a double delusion: 1) that we already know our partner as fully as possible and 2) we are incredibly similar and well matched. Ridiculous!

The truth is that we know our partner less well when the relationship is beginning, and our knowledge of each other grows deeper and better over time. And because of the first delusion, we have little basis to conclude that we are well-matched because we only know each other superficially and partially, at first.

Well, let's apply this to our children. I think we often try to convince ourselves that our children will and should have the same values we do. They should care about the same things we care about. One of the great traditions in parenting is to try to manufacture a bunch of "values clones."

This is silly. Each of our children is a separate and unique human being. They only have about half of our genetic make-up (unless they are adopted or step-children, in which case they have none), and their life experiences are far different than our own. So they couldn't be copies of us anyway, as genetics and experience are the two major factors in shaping a person.

As values are a central part of our character, what does this tell us about raising children of character? First, don't unfairly expect children to hold the exact same values you do. It will never happen. Second, be sure to focus on the important values (moral/ethical values) that have to do with elements including human rights, fairness, respect, caring, and responsibility. Dig in your heels on those, but cut kids some slack on the values that are more negotiable, like tastes in music or clothing.

And third, be sure to talk about values. The other day my son announced to me that he thinks it is a waste of money to buy a nice house and fill it with nice furniture (something we have been doing for the past two years, apparently much to his chagrin). He is also not impressed with our efforts to put away money for his college education. He would much rather spend the money on electronic equipment (for him), clothing (for him), and eventually a car (for him). Clearly, we disagree on how to spend the family's hard-earned money. But we discuss it. And that's how I know his values differ from mine (although in this case, not by much).

If you want to raise kids of character, recognize that their character will never be exactly what you want or expect. But they deserve your respect, nonetheless. And merely talking about values is a fine way to build character, and that is something you should value.

Open the Door

WHEN WE LIVED IN BERLIN MANY YEARS AGO, MY WIFE and I enjoyed noticing little differences between the German culture and our own. Such as the use of real candles on Christmas trees, taking off your shoes when you enter a house, and closing the doors to all rooms in the house. This closing of doors bothered me. It seemed very antisocial to me.

Recently my son was having some trouble with his schoolwork. He didn't seem to understand some of his math assignments. But my wife and I didn't know it, because we had lapsed into a pattern where, when it was time for my son to begin his homework, he went into his room and closed his door. We didn't hear from him again until he was done, exhausted, hungry for dinner, or thirsty.

I didn't like his door being closed so much. I suppose I felt the same way as in Berlin—shut out, separated, excluded—but I have more sense than to go into a cross between a teen lion's den and a rat's nest. So I made some snide comments every now and then and let it go at that.

When tests were imminent and he began to really worry about how he would perform, he emerged like a bear from hibernation, blinking at the light of day, for he seems to prefer doing his homework by the faint light of his computer screen. So we gathered at the kitchen table and I began to help him study. He would proclaim utter mastery, I would test him, he would fail miserably, and he would sullenly go back to studying. Then the cycle would repeat, but with him getting better and better each time until he seemed ready for the exam.

As usual, I was less than patient, he was surly, we battled, but he learned. Not what I would consider the epitome of a relaxing time, but very productive. And when we were done, he thanked me and seemed to genuinely recognize that he learned the material much better interactively than barricaded in the dark, gloomy laundry basket he calls his room.

There are a couple of things to note here. First, he recognized on his own that this method of studying and preparing together worked. Second, he thanked me. Third, he actually did better on his exam. Fourth, this was a notable interaction for both of us, and, I think, added to the parent-child bond. Fifth, I was modeling helping behavior (although not particularly graciously, unfortunately).

I just returned home from his eighth-grade graduation. In his welcoming remarks, the superintendent of his school district pointed out that as kids enter high school, parents tend to pull back from involvement in school. This is true. But he also argued that kids need their parents' involvement even more in high school. He implored us to stay involved in our kids' schooling over the next four years. I intend to.

So open the door. Not just to the room, but to the relationship, and to helping your children, especially your teens. They may not reach out and they may even push you away, but inside, they want you to be there for them. They may close the door, so it is your job to open it.

How to "Talk Good"

YOU'VE PROBABLY SEEN THOSE EXCELLENT PUBLIC service announcements telling you that talking to your children about drugs is one of the best ways to prevent them from engaging in substance use. Well, talking to your child about right and wrong in general is no different. One of the best ways to foster healthy character development in children is by "talking good."

But like most recipes for child development, this is easier said than done. A parent can talk about ethical issues in ways that are helpful or in ways that actually hurt character development. Some of this is obvious. Ranting and raving at a child is obviously not an effective way to foster character development. Nor is avoiding the topic completely. So what can a parent do to effectively "talk good"?

The first rule is to make sure that you openly and honestly present your important values. Tell kids what you stand for. As Dr. Thomas Lickona, author of *Raising Good Children* (a highly recommended book for parents), has said, "Practice what you preach, but preach what you practice." In other words, be sure to not forget to tell kids about those things for which you care deeply.

However, it is also important that kids have a "voice." They need to be encouraged to contribute to the discussion, whether it is merely to repeat and agree, or even to question, challenge, and analyze. Two important things happen in such cases. Most obvious is that kids get their messages, feelings, and ideas heard. And those ideas are challenged and challenge others. This intellectual tussling is what builds mature moral thinking. But perhaps even more important, they learn that they and their perspectives are valued, are taken seriously by their parents. They learn that their parents care about who they are, what they stand for, and what is important to them. They learn that they are players in the game of life, and most particularly in their family, which is the primary place where character is formed.

Of course, you have to talk to kids at their level. You can't tell a five-year-old to be a "good citizen" or to engage in "distributive justice." But you can tell him to "help out" and to be "fair" and to "share."

Throughout all of this, parents need to be emotionally supportive. The child should never doubt that she is cared about and loved. If the intellectual tussling and discussing is what nurtures moral thinking, the emotional support is the soil in which it grows. Cold antagonism cannot nourish the roots of character development.

And it is okay to disagree. In fact, disagreement is inevitable. You won't always see eye to eye with your children, but they must feel safe to disagree and still feel that they are loved. This does not mean you should lie and act as if you agree with your child when you honestly don't. Rather, simply acknowledge the disagreement, present your case, hear your child's viewpoint, and if no resolution is on the horizon, agree to disagree. This is no different than what we should do with our partners.

So when Johnny or Nancy says, "I don't believe in God" or "What's a homosexual?" or "I think they should kill people who are mean to cats," parents need to talk with them about issues. Parents should not just lecture, nor should they sweep the difficult issues under the table. Instead, they need to talk to their children and make it known that their points of view are valued. But parents should also speak in a way that openly discloses their own values.

In fact, parents should be looking for such opportunities. Don't wait for the inevitable, challenging statements and questions by your child. Raise them yourselves. Dinner tables are there for conversation, not just eating; it should be family time. And family time should be open, supportive, and challenging conversation time. If your family doesn't look like this...well, talk about it.

Telling It Like It Is

ONE OF THE GREATEST CAUSES OF PROBLEMS BETWEEN people is communication. It certainly seems as if our communication functions could have at least been designed better, then we wouldn't have so many problems "relating to each other." We wouldn't have so many misunderstandings. This doesn't just apply when we talk to other adults either—it also applies when talking to our kids.

Take for instance "induction." What, you may ask, is that and why would you do it to a child? Well, it is one of those well-rounded and well-established recipes for good character. It is explaining your parenting (or teaching) behavior to children, and doing so with a special focus on the consequences of their behavior, particularly the consequences for hurting others' feelings.

> Induction...is explaining your parenting (or teaching) behavior to children, and doing so with a special focus on the consequences of their behavior, such as the consequences for hurting others' feelings.

It may sound a bit technical, but it is really quite simple. When punishing Tom for taking a toy from Annie, you don't just yell at him or give him a time out. Instead, you tell him that you are giving him a time out because he took the toy and, that by doing so, made Annie very sad. In fact, that's why she's crying. Or instead of simply hugging Roger for saying thank you to Aunt Mary, you tell Roger that you are so proud of him for his good manners and that they made Aunt Mary very happy. That's induction.

Why bother adding the explanation to your behavior? Because research has repeatedly shown that doing so leads to all kinds of positive outcomes for kids' development. Kids are more generous, are better able to reason about right and wrong, are more empathic, and have a more fully developed conscience.

It also reduces a lot of the frustration that breeds parent-child conflicts. I remember a holiday gathering at my brother-in-law's house years ago. My niece, Wendy (then about three years old), was so wound up, she was getting into everything. When her mother warned her for the third or fourth time to leave the kitchen, Wendy smarted-off to her. Her mom yelled at her for being "fresh" and ordered her to go downstairs. Downstairs was only three steps away, but Wendy only made it halfway as she collapsed in a sobbing heap on the second step. I was an advanced doctoral student in child psychology back then, so I ignored it. But my wife, far more sensitive and perceptive than I, asked Wendy if she knew what "fresh" meant. She didn't. Once my wife explained it, Wendy perked up and went on her merry way. When she understood it, she could readily own up to it and move on. But when she had no idea why she was being punished, she couldn't. And we know that parents who routinely do this have kids who are more helpful and caring.

So take the time to "tell it like it is." A little induction goes a long way in helping to foster good character.

Listening for Success

IT IS VERY DIFFICULT TO FIGURE OUT IF ALL THE WORK you are doing to raise kids of character is actually paying off. First of all, you are far less of an objective observer. I remember a birthday message my mother wrote to me when I was a pre-teen. It read something like this: "Happy birthday to the most wonderful, intelligent, handsome, kind, creative boy I know. From an unbiased observer, your mother."

Second, our kids, like every other human ever to walk this planet, are pretty complicated beings.

Third, they tend to act quite differently with their parents than they do with others. You all have probably gotten glowing feedback

> **There are ways to assess how your child is doing—probably the best indicator is how they consistently behave when they don't think you are watching.**

from another parent or adult who supervised your child or observed him playing at their house. And you wondered how they could have confused your little devil with some apparently angelic other child.

Fourth, we never know for sure which signs are relevant and which are not. Is the current temper tantrum a true indicator of your child's character, or is the spontaneous hug she gave you more indicative? My advice on this one is not to overemphasize any single instance of behavior. Look for patterns.

Despite all these barriers, there are ways to assess how your child is doing. Probably the best indicator is how they consistently behave when they don't think you are watching.

Now I am not recommending spying or eavesdropping. That could backfire and destroy the fragile trust between parent and child. Keep your nose out of their diary. Don't pick up the other phone extension to listen to their conversations. You don't have to. There will be plenty of opportunities to observe; you just have to pay attention. With the little ones, this is a no-brainer. They are so egocentric that they can quickly forget that you are in sight or listening range.

But even teenagers drop their guards periodically and show their true colors. My son and I frequently debate (read: argue) about the type of music he listens to, mostly about the messages in some of the music. I argue that he shouldn't consume and support hateful, violent, anti-social lyrics. He argues that it won't affect him. For free speech. And so on. Then he laments his misfortune in getting stuck with a dad who is into character education and ethics and moral psychology.

Recently, however, he was in the car and his girlfriend was in the back seat while I was driving. He was playing one of his annoying CDs. He skipped over a song as it began. His girlfriend asked him to play it. He said "I don't think my dad would like that. Don't you know what he does for a living?" When she answered "a teacher" he corrected her and said "No, he is a professor of morality. And I don't think he would like to listen to a song about mass murder, do you?"

I shut my mouth but kept my ears wide open. Despite all of the posturing with me to defend such music, when he was talking to someone else, he took a much more enlightened position. My message seemed to have taken at least a fledgling hold. I would never have guessed that from our conversations. But simply *listening* gave me a perspective on parenting for character success that I might not have gotten otherwise.

So keep your eyes and ears open for signs of success. If you parent wisely and listen well, you will hear the sounds of character growing all around you.

It's What's Inside That Counts

KIDS NOT ONLY SAY THE DARNDEST THINGS, THEY ALSO *think* them. And you often won't know unless you ask and listen. It is not uncommon for kids to come up with some fairly bizarre ideas about the world, especially, but not exclusively, young children.

I have been told by parents and teachers about some surprising ideas that kids have come up with about the 9/11 terrorist disaster. One child came home from school to announce that some bad men had driven planes into the World Trade Center towers and hurt a lot of people. That was pretty accurate until she added that there was now a "state war between Florida and Pennsylvania." If we don't talk to our kids about how they understand the world and what they think they know, we will not be able to dispel such misconceptions.

> If we don't talk to our kids about how they understand the world and what they think they know, we will not be able to dispel their misconceptions.

Another child had been watching the television coverage of the terrorist attacks for a few days and, when asked by his parents what he knew about it, proclaimed that people had attacked America with airplanes and were still doing it. His parents realized that the repetitive replays of the airplanes hitting the World Trade Center had been construed as continued attacks rather than video repeats of the 9/11 attacks. Think of how frightening such attacks are for a young child, but how much more terrifying if they think they are relentlessly continuing for days or weeks. Having to fear reality is bad enough. Children don't need to needlessly fear their misconceptions as well.

And it is not just major events that produce such misunderstandings. One parent told me that his son suddenly began staying up night after night and asking for one glass of water after another. It took a bit of questioning but they discovered that his reasoning went as follows. They had run out of gas in the car recently and his dad had explained that "the car had died because it ran out of gas." The same day, his dad mentioned that he had "gas" from drinking too much. The boy had figured out that if he ran out of gas he would die, just as the car had, so he stayed up all night drinking to save his own life.

It is not just young children who misconstrue the world like this. One adolescent boy told me that people shouldn't keep promises. When I asked why, he told me that older kids might make you promise to steal something from a store. And if you do, they will make you promise to do worse things and you could end up in jail. Now, I never would have thought of a promise in this way, but I didn't grow up in a crime-ridden, gang-infested neighborhood as he did.

So don't just listen to your kids, *truly* listen, and ask them what they think and what they know. Ask them how they feel about things. Ask them why they seem afraid or confused, and so on. This will help you short-circuit their unsubstantiated fears and inaccurate beliefs. And it is also another opportunity to simply talk to your kids about what they care about.

Watch Your Mouth

I SWEAR I TRY TO WATCH MY MOUTH. REALLY. WHEN MY son was first born, I made a list of the behaviors I engage in that I didn't want him to copy, and there were many. One of them was using foul language.

Just so you don't think I am generally coarse and vulgar, I was 36 years old and had spent much time on sports teams, in locker rooms, and in theater dressing rooms (working, not lurking). I was quite used to coarse language and off-color humor. I never used such language when it was inappropriate, but I was afraid I would do it at home and my son would pick it up. So I vowed to clean up my language at home and this spilled over to other venues. To show the power of such behavior, I want to recount two situations.

The first was when my son was a toddler and first learning to talk. I was in the kitchen, and my son was doing what he did best: toddling under my feet. I dropped a raw egg on the kitchen floor, making a mess. Without thinking, I yelled an expletive.

The next thing I heard was a little voice behind me hollering "Sh*t. Sh*t. Sh*t...." He had no idea what it meant, but he heard it, liked it, and appropriated it for his own edification and language enrichment.

The second incident happened recently. I regularly play soccer on Sunday evenings in a men's over-40, over-fed league. The evening's game was nearly over. I made a great run on the ball, poked it away from the opposing player and took off down the sideline. I was flying toward the goal (well, compared with the other over-40, over-fed players, it *looked* like I was moving fast), when it felt like a sniper had shot me in the leg. I went down like a deer shot in full stride. From past experience, I knew before I hit the ground that I had ripped my hamstring muscle. Partly in pain and partly in frustration, I screamed out a familiar abbreviation of "firetruck."

After being assisted off the field, I noticed that one of my fellow player's daughters (about 10 years old) was on the sideline watching this whole affair. My first reaction was regret at having cursed. So, with an icepack on my leg, and still in pain and despair (mainly because I knew I would miss a couple of weeks of soccer), I called her over and apologized to her for swearing.

I reasoned that it was the best I could do to undo the damage of modeling poor character. I hope she got the message—I certainly did. And in case you didn't, watch your mouth so your children won't have to watch theirs.

Kind Words

DID YOU EVER NOTICE HOW GOOD YOU FEEL WHEN someone compliments you? And how bad you feel when someone points out your faults, especially in a not-so-nice way? And whom do you want to hang out with, the person who put you down or the person who built you up?

Everyone else feels that way too, including your children. They feel miserable when you call them names, yell at them, criticize them, or in other ways tear them down. They feel that after such a session, it's all their fault. And they feel great and want to hang with you and hug you when you tell them how proud you are of them, or how nice they look, or what a nice thing they did for someone else. Just like you would feel if you were in their shoes.

Hal Urban is a retired high school teacher from San Francisco who has written a wonderful book called *Life's Greatest Lessons: 20 Things I Want My Kids to Know.* In his book is a chapter called "Kind words cost little, but accomplish much." And now he has a new book entirely on this topic: *Positive Words, Powerful Results.* He makes the point about how effective it is to go out of your way to say kind things to others. In other words, to affirm them.

You probably know—or better yet are—someone who gets along with most people. Has loads of friends, and is someone everyone seems to enjoy being around.

What is the secret? Research into friendships, marriages, and social interactions suggests that it results partly from being a kind and affirming person, being positive and complimentary.

Now, of course, it has to be sincere. Most people will quickly see through false flattery, even if we still like to receive the compliment. Many communication experts will teach you to begin a critical feedback message with a compliment. First tell someone what you admire about them or their work before you tell them what you feel needs improvement.

Healthy, positive relationships are the foundation for character building. Children develop healthy, positive character only if they experience loving, safe, nurturing relationships.

It is difficult to build such relationships on harsh words and put-downs. Kind words do indeed accomplish much, including fostering your kid's healthy character.

Control

Whose Problem Is It, Anyway?

ONE OF THE THINGS THAT MAKE WRITING THIS COLUMN easy is the fact that I make so many mistakes. I simply list all the errors I make as a parent, then transform them into lessons, and offer advice to my readers.

When we have a problem in our home, I usually slip into my know-it-all, problem-solver mode and offer the solution. And that's not always a good thing to do.

Because of my educational background and training, schools frequently engage me as a consultant for the purpose of developing programs to foster students' character development. From time to time, I notice that school staff members make the same mistake I do—rushing forward with a solution rather than allowing their students to give it a try.

> **Shared authority promotes growth of responsibility and problem-solving skills. It also builds relationships and a sense of the whole for both the school and the classroom.**

A teacher recently told me that her second-grade boys were stuffing paper towels in the urinals, causing the bathroom to flood. She had tried implementing various rules, such as only one boy in the bathroom at a time, but nothing seemed to work.

I told her that perhaps it wasn't her responsibility to solve the problem; instead, maybe she should think of it as a problem that belonged to the students. I suggested she ask them to come up with a solution. And she did just that—she asked her students to find a way to stop the bathroom misbehavior. Much to her surprise, the students came back with something that worked. They decided to elect respected, responsible peers to serve as bathroom monitors. And sure enough, after 40 days and 40 nights of daily floods, the bathroom waters subsided.

Was it a miracle? Not really. Schools often experience problems concerning bathrooms, recess, cafeterias, transportation—wherever students congregate. Generally speaking, administrators assume they "own" all problems, and that every problem that arises in the school must be resolved by them, so they attempt to come up with solutions that sometimes don't work. I suggest that in certain circumstances, school administrators redefine the issue of problem *ownership*, asking the students for help in finding the solutions to problems or issues that affect them and their environment.

This is not only a matter of efficiency in problem solving; it's also a matter of character development. Shared authority promotes growth of responsibility and problem-solving skills. It also builds relationships and a sense of the whole for both the school and the classroom. And it helps our children prepare for their eventual roles as adults in a community, where responsible behavior by its members contributes to the safety and well-being of all.

The concept can also be utilized by families. When a family problem arises, the parents need not rush in and claim ownership for solving it. What is this great desire to own problems, anyway? I would much rather own something nice. Wouldn't you?

Instead, share ownership of problems. Assign to your kids the responsibility for finding a workable solution. They'll be pleased that you considered them to be so capable and they'll be far more likely to adhere to the solution because it was their own. Remember that responsibility breeds even greater responsibility. And responsibility is a core aspect of good character.

Getting Your Priorities Straight

MULTI-TASKING IS NOT A GREAT STRENGTH OF MANY parents, so we get in a rut. We focus on an issue and stick with it, not noticing the collateral damage we are doing by ignoring more important tasks.

I know I do this all the time. Last night at dinner, my son, in his inimitable culinary style, began picking apart his food, looking for any part of it that seemed suspicious to him. This drives me crazy. So, being an expert in child development, I yelled at him.

A bit later in the meal he said, "Why do you care if I just eat the parts of food that I like?" He was right. What was the big deal, after all?

> It was my wife's caution that truly woke me up, in that I was sacrificing my relationship with my son for trivial battles.

Now, that is a relatively minor example. But I'll bet you can think of plenty of your own pet peeves that you inflict on your children. And many of them may be justified. After all, he does waste food this way. And he tends to reject much nutritious food in favor of processed junk. Is my bias showing again?

But the point is not whether you can justify your point. It is whether this is a battle worth fighting. And at what cost?

I remember vividly early in my dating relationship with my wife when we had a big break-up. Somehow I had the wisdom to realize that when we next saw each other I had two choices: 1) make a big deal of the break-up and lament all the grief we were experiencing or 2) force myself to ignore that and just try to have a really great time together. Even more out of character for me, I chose number two. And it worked—we have been married for over 30 years.

Recently, my wife pointed out that I had been relentlessly nit-picking my son about every thing he did with which I disagreed, and it was clearly taking a toll on both of us. We were not happy separately and we surely were not happy together.

My wife suggested I use the old tried-and-true strategy of trying to just have a good time together with my son. Just have fun. So I did. We go out to eat together and just talk. We go to movies together. We go shopping together. And just enjoy each other's company. And that pretty much took care of that problem.

But it was my wife's caution that truly woke me up, in that I was sacrificing my relationship with my son for trivial battles. I was winning the battles and losing the war. I was in danger of driving my son away from me.

It is sometimes important to step back and get the big picture to get your parenting priorities straight. Because, although it is not enough by itself, building a relationship on love is critical to raising good children. And remember, you cannot browbeat your children into good character, nor should you want to. Character is born out of trust and love, and it is these that should be cultivated, as you help them to grow.

Father Doesn't Always Know Best

I AM A PRETTY SELF-ASSURED PERSON. I HAVE A PH.D. I write a newspaper column. I am well-respected in my profession. I am pretty smart. (I'd better stop there. I suspect you are already starting to hate me.)

My wife and son take much of the brunt of this self-assuredness. And I am pretty good at arguing my side of an issue, so I often win. Well, at least I often win the battle.

I am less confident that this strategy is helping me win the war. The battle is the particular argument—the war is the relationship with others and how they perceive me. I may win the arguments with my son, but if the cost is alienating or hurting him, then this particular tactic is not successful. Besides, we know that kids grow up to be like us, and we don't want them to develop our bad habits and character.

I was recently told a story about an elementary school child who had learned through a character development program at school to believe in yourself and persevere. To be optimistic and have a "can do" attitude. He was helping his mother decorate the Christmas tree when she accidentally dropped a treasured family heirloom ornament, which smashed into many fragments.

Mom was despondent that she had destroyed the ornament. Her young son, invoking the character lessons at school, suggested they fix the ornament. Mom, of course, knowing better, said it was impossible. Her son, however, remained undaunted and recited the lessons from school that said you can do whatever you set your mind to. Mom resisted. Son persisted. Mom relented and they set about to try to do what mom knew was a futile repair job.

Lo and behold, they did manage to resurrect the ornament. Son was vindicated and mom was relieved. Son knows best in this case.

I can clearly see the delight and surprise on my son's face, even now that he is in high school, when he is right about something and I am wrong. Even about the most trivial issue.

There is a sense of power and self-esteem that comes from being right. Especially when in disagreement with someone who seems to be right more often than not. Like arrogant old dad.

Remember that you are not always right. Kids may sometimes know things or figure things out better than you, so keep an open mind and an open ear. This will build communication, a positive relationship, and the kid's self-esteem, initiative, and character. Trust me, I am confident about this one.

Power Trip

POWER AND CONTROL ARE ISSUES IN ALL RELATIONSHIPS, including parent-child relationships—just think about your relationships with your parents and you will see what I mean. So it is helpful to examine how power and control affect the way we raise, or fail to raise, our kids, and how that affects their character.

Especially, but not exclusively, with young children, there is a continual tug of war. On the one hand, the kids have two basic needs: autonomy and belongingness. Autonomy refers to the need to be independent, to control one's own life and behavior, to have the upper hand, to strive and to win. Belongingness refers to the need to be emotionally bonded, to be attached, to be part of a relationship. Serving these two masters is a true challenge.

Kids have two basic needs: autonomy and belongingness.

In order to serve autonomy, the kids resist us, defy us, challenge us, argue with us, and are downright ornery and stubborn. But to serve belongingness they comply, acquiesce, and give in. This makes them unpredictable and unfathomable.

But let us not forget that even as adults, we have the same needs. Starting to sound a bit like a psychological bull fight, isn't it?

It is our job to try to pick our way through this psychological minefield to navigate a course that is best for our children. This takes reflection, insight, compassion, and self-sacrifice.

One of the tricky tasks of parenting is to wield control appropriately. Let's take a look at some reasons we fail to do so. First, there are the cases where we are serving our own needs. For example, perhaps you have a need to have more control in your life.

Your boss is oppressive and your need for control is not being met there. Or your spouse is exercising the same behavior, and you feel that you never get your way. So you over-control your kids to find some space in your life to be lord and master.

On the other hand, perhaps you feel that you didn't love your parent(s) enough, and are afraid your child won't love you. So you fear being domineering and eventually losing their love. As a result, you under-control your kids and let them run wild and rule the roost.

Second, you have a theory. Everyone has them, what we sometimes call implicit theories. This means we act according to the theory, but don't realize that we are doing so. Some folks think, for instance, that physical punishment is the most effective way to control kids' behavior. They are wrong, but they *think* it is so, and therefore they slap and beat and spank their kids to get compliance. This may, to them, work in the short term by getting immediate compliance, but it doesn't work to build good character in the long run, which is what counts.

Others think that trying to control kids at all breaks their spirit, so they let the kids run wild in the household and get their way a good percentage of the time. They, too, are wrong. Kids need adults to set expectations and standards for them. And to be in control, so the kids feel safe and protected.

It is not just the unintelligent or uneducated or mentally ill parents who do this—some of my best friends, people who are smart and kind and caring, make these mistakes. I know a new mom who is also a pediatrician, who seems allergic to saying "no" to her infant son. I make these same mistakes all the time as well, and I have a Ph.D. in child development. One of my favorite professors when I was a student told me that all she learned in school went out the window as soon as she had her own kids.

So here's to keeping the window closed and hanging on to the good advice for the sake of our kids' character. Kids need parents who can put their feet down, who can say no, who can hold the line, who can set reasonable and well-justified standards. But those parents also have to be self-aware, thoughtful, and caring, and they have to recognize when it is appropriate to let kids have control as well.

For those of you who are afraid to control and say no, remember that your child's character depends upon your showing them the right path, consistently transmitting your values, and making them feel safe and protected. And those who over-control and dominate their children must learn that they need to feel a sense of autonomy, to be in control of their own lives, and to learn how to negotiate and collaborate with others.

This is the true art of parenting, and it is a lifelong challenge, something you will never feel comes naturally. It is hard work to build good character.

Holidays

All-Year Cheer

ONE OF THE ODD THINGS ABOUT THE HOLIDAY SEASON is the change in how people treat each other. On the one hand, they try to get into the "holiday spirit." They try to be especially cheerful, pleasant, and tolerant. There is more smiling, more hugging, more giving.

On the other hand, they end up stressed out by all the smiling, all the hugging, all the giving...and all the buying. Nerves get frazzled and the "holiday spirit" begins to seem like a burden.

The whole notion of turning niceness on and off is a bit puzzling to me. I was a mail carrier (mailman to most of you) when I was in graduate school. I was the new kid to the post office, so I was broken in as the fill-in guy. I was assigned the route of whoever was on vacation that week. So I got to see lots of areas of Detroit as I rotated through the different routes. This was the mid-1970s when Detroit was, sadly, the "murder capital" of the United States. There were many neighborhoods in which I was rather hesitant to go. Of course, those were precisely the neighborhoods to which I was sent.

> Let's get rid of holiday spirit—and *replace* it with basic human kindness that knows no season and no boundaries, all year round.

But something amazing happened. Everyone was nice to me (well, except for the dogs, but that's another column—suffice it to say, it was funny sight to see me trying to shake the poodle off my pants leg or involved in a "High Noon" stand-off with a chihuahua in the middle of the street, armed only with a can of "Halt").

It seemed that everyone wanted to be friendly to the mailman, because the mailman brings us things we want. People also are obsessed with talking about the weather to him. "Nice day, eh?" "Looks like rain, don't you think?" "Sure is a hot one." And so on.

During this time, I didn't look like a mailman because they didn't issue a uniform until after 89 days of work. This was during my hippie era, so I was dressed in jeans and t-shirt, and I had wild, frizzy hair. The only giveaway was the mailbag, but that seemed enough to alert all the dogs.

We have a tendency to choose the people to be nice to and our times to be nice. We are nice to mail carriers and UPS delivery men. We are nice to our grandmothers. And we are nice at holiday season.

Here's a crazy notion: Why not be nice all the time? To everyone? Let me be another Scrooge. I say let's get rid of the holiday spirit— and *replace* it with basic human kindness that knows no season and no boundaries, all year round.

By doing so, we'll teach our kids to have good character not just at certain times of the year and in certain situations and with certain people. We'll teach them good character by demonstrating the power of all-year cheer. This my holiday gift—and my wish—to each of you.

What's the Point?

MANY OF OUR SHARED TRADITIONS—WHETHER CIVIC, religious, ethnic, or personal—have deep meaning. There is a point to Martin Luther King Day, Thanksgiving, Christmas, family reunions, etc. And we often forget these points.

Someone I work with recently told me that she discourages gift-giving within the family at Christmas and instead encourages family acts of charity. I imagine that her child frowns upon this anomalous family tradition. It likely appears to her kid that his parents have missed the point—that the rest of the world understands the true tradition of Christmas, namely getting gifts. But this family has found a way to truly focus on one of the real messages of their faith tradition: charity.

> We tend to lose too many of the fundamental values and beliefs that form the foundation for the best that humans have conceived and created.

Many traditions are specifically about remembering a moral message. For instance, the Jewish holiday of Passover has within it the requirement to retell the story of Exodus so it is never forgotten. Some Native American traditions likewise focus on oral storytelling to pass traditions down through generations.

These are wonderful ways of keeping alive sacred truths and deep meanings. We tend to lose too many of the fundamental values and beliefs that form the foundation for the best that humans have conceived and created. It is difficult in a materialistic society like ours to miss the message that having things is a fundamental good—that wealth equals virtue. So we have to work extra hard to get kids to learn that the point of the George Washington cherry tree story is the importance of truth-telling—not how cool it would be to have an axe and cut down trees.

Our children are not born knowing the power of truth or the importance of collaboration, so we need to teach them. We must look to our respective traditions and figure out what they truly stand for, as well as explore our enduring traditions and their deep and powerful points of meaning. Why do we celebrate Thanksgiving? What is the real point of Christmas or Hanukkah or Ramadan? Why do we go to the trouble of arranging family gatherings on holidays? Why do we keep telling certain stories over and over?

The values that underlie so many of our traditions are fragile flames. They can light the path to good character and to a fair and caring world. Or they can be extinguished in the winds created by our headlong rushing to buy this and get that and be the first to arrive there.

So take some time at every tradition to talk about its underlying message and the reasons for it. Create your own traditions that support those points, like engaging in charity at Christmas instead of just consuming more, or sharing thanks with others at Thanksgiving. Use the opportunities that traditions present to reflect and teach.

Our kids will never know goodness if we don't do it and talk about it and, like the Olympic torch that crosses America every four years, pass the flame from generation to generation.

Modeling
and Heroes

Whom Do You Admire?

I RECENTLY HAD THE WONDERFUL OPPORTUNITY TO SEE one of my heroes in the flesh. Often our heroes are not available to us because they are historical figures, or they live in worlds, such as sports or television, that we don't inhabit. But sometimes a hero is available to us if it is a friend, family member, or mentor. When your hero is only infrequently available, it is important to see or meet or hear that person when the rare opportunity arises.

One of my heroes is Morris Dees, the founder of the Southern Poverty Law Center. Dees grew up in rural Alabama and, as a lawyer, has

> [Morris Dees] is my hero because he has dedicated his life to serving the disadvantaged, and to thwarting the hateful and violent actions of bigots. He is also my hero because he does this with humility and courage....

made it his life's work to fight racism, hate crimes, and prejudice. His organization is one that I have long supported with charitable contributions. He is my hero because he has dedicated his life to serving the disadvantaged, and to thwarting the hateful and violent actions of bigots. He is also my hero because he does this with humility and courage, for his life is constantly threatened and attacks have been numerous.

I admired him because of his reputation; I had neither seen him nor spoken to him. I didn't know if he was young or old, short or tall, black or white, Christian or Jew, but when I learned he was coming to my city to speak, I knew I had to go to hear and see him, no matter how busy I was. I arranged a break in my day and drove down to the Graham Chapel at Washington University in St. Louis. I went alone and found a seat in the packed room. He was eloquent, soft-spoken, humble, and powerful. When he was introduced, he received a standing ovation and I rose to join the audience, tears in my eyes. I knew then that he represented what I believed in; that he *deserved* to be my hero and that he was a purveyor of justice and goodness. I suddenly felt what I had only known.

So I challenge you to first reflect on your personal heroes. Who are they? And then to consider why you admire them—are they worthy of your admiration? Do you admire them because they're handsome and rich, or because they live out values that you cherish in their own beliefs and behavior?

If you can, support your heroes in their work. If not, write a letter expressing appreciation for what your hero means to you. Try to meet or hear or see them. If that is not possible, study them. When I was a faculty member at Marquette University, I would routinely nominate my various heroes to receive an honorary degree so I could meet them. Alas, none of them were ever chosen. I think the late Fred Rogers and Pete Seeger would have made fine honorary degree recipients.

But even that is not enough. You also need to share your heroes. This column is one way I can do that, but I also try to share them with my son as a way to show him what I value in a person. I have told him about my contributions to Morris Dees' organization. I have told him about Morris Dees himself, and I told him about going to hear him speak and why it was important to me.

But as I sat in the chapel listening to Dees, I realized that I had stopped one step short—I should have brought my son with me. I should have taken him out of school for this important lesson in life.

Choose your heroes wisely, then share them with your children. Let your children know the things about your heroes' character that you admire. In this way, you will be helping to develop your child into someone you and others will admire. For you never know—your child may one day become someone's hero.

Do as I Say AND as I Do

DO YOU TELL YOUR KIDS WHAT YOU THINK IS RIGHT AND wrong? Probably. It is hard to be a parent and not lecture, preach, or teach much of the time. I know I do it.

You should do it, too. It's important to let your kids know what is important to you. What you think is good character and what you think is not. To teach right from wrong. But one mistake we frequently make is to tell kids to "do as I say, not as I do." Sound familiar?

Kids are great at catching your hypocrisy. They will frequently notice and point it out when you violate your own rules and lessons. Even toddlers will wisely identify your behavior as a "no-no." And it gets worse as they get older. In the later elementary school years, they will lord it over you when you eat what you tell them not to eat. Or when you use a swear word that you have forbidden them from uttering. And adolescents have a field day torturing you with such observations.

My son is approaching driver's license age (consider yourself forewarned; it might be a good time to reinforce the concrete on your houses and lock your children in the basement or buy a Humvee and load it with sandbags). So he monitors my driving. He smugly points out that I do not come to a full stop at stop signs. That I am driving over the speed limit. That I failed to signal for a lane change.

In fact, I am beginning to think that I am the worst driver on the planet, and he was sent here to torture me into forfeiting my driver's license.

And so I feel a great tension. After all, I drive a standard transmission car, and it is much easier to nearly stop and then move forward at a stop sign than having to shift down to first gear for a complete stop. And when no one is in the next lane, who is harmed by not signaling? Right.

On the other hand, shouldn't I be practicing what I preach? And then it hits me. I can invoke that saving phrase that all parents handily keep up their sleeves. "Do as I say and not as I do."

However, that does not work. First of all, we know that children are more likely to copy your behavior than follow your verbal lessons. In other words, they are more likely to do as you do and not as you say—just the opposite of what you wanted.

A recent study in *Preventive Medicine* looked at high school girls' smoking behavior and its relation to their parents' smoking, as well as their mothers' messages and attitudes about smoking. A mother telling her daughter not to smoke was quite effective in reducing the daughter's smoking (in fact, it cut it almost in half). But only if her parents did not smoke.

If the parents *were* smokers, however, the mother's antismoking attitudes and messages made absolutely no difference in the daughter's behavior. In other words, kids only do as you say if *you* do as you say.

Smoking is a form of self-abuse. It is considered to be one of the "gateway" drugs that opens the door to other drug use. So this example is an important one.

Character educators are beginning to understand that character education is a form of primary prevention for all sorts of harmful behaviors, not only smoking. Parents need to understand that parenting for character also helps prevent dangerous, risky behavior. And one important form of parenting for character is to "do as you say" so your kids will do likewise.

Mirror, Mirror...

WANT TO KNOW WHAT YOUR KID WILL GROW UP TO BE like? Then look in the mirror. Look *closely*. That is what your kid is most likely to end up like. Well, not *exactly* like you, as there are too many other influences in kids' lives. But kids' characters are in large part determined by how the important people around them act. And parents are *the* most important people around kids, for better or for worse.

Not only can you influence your children by the behaviors you model, but you will, and you must. Their future depends on it, and therefore so does the future of the world. The character development of today's children determines the character of society's next generation. Today's kids are tomorrow's leaders, followers, saints, and sinners.

Many people hope to compensate for their misdeeds by preaching the right message. "Smoking is a filthy habit, dear, and I will quit as soon as I can," a mother preaches as she smokes a cigarette. "I don't want you to end up a loser like me," a dad mourns as the police lead him away. "I am so angry with you for hitting Susie in school today. Don't you ever hit her again," a mom screams as she spanks her son.

I hate to burst this bubble of self-delusion, but it doesn't work that way. We know from research that kids learn more from what you do than from what you say. These kids are more likely to smoke, break the law, and hit others than to do the opposite, despite their parents' impassioned pleas. They will follow in their parents' footsteps; the abused often become the abusers. The child you just spanked has learned to hit others when she's upset with their behavior, despite mom's rhetorical warning against it.

And when kids hear one message and watch another, they are

receiving mixed messages, confusing the kids and leading them further astray.

So what to do? If kids are watching—and they are, probably more then you think—then clean up your act. Even better, clean it up full time, regardless of who is watching. One of the simple ethical guidelines is to ask yourself whether you would be as comfortable with a behavior if your mother were watching, or if it were to be announced on the front page of your local paper. More important for your children, ask yourself if you would want them emulating the same behavior.

Think of all the times you found yourself using the same phrases your mother and father used in punishing you when you were a child. Phrases that you hated and vowed never to use. Don't call an exorcist; it is a normal product of the awesome power of parental modeling. Instead, clean up your language, treat others with respect, tell the truth, help others in need, follow the Golden Rule, take responsibility for your actions, try to leave the world a better place than it was when you entered it. In other words, be a super model.

Time-Out for Parents

ONE OF THE GREAT INVENTIONS IN CONTROLLING children's behavior is the "time-out." It is difficult to be a parent in this day and age without using time-outs, especially with toddlers and pre-schoolers. Such a response to kids' tantrums, noncompliance, aggression, and other negative behaviors serves as a removal from harm, time to cool down, and an opportunity to reflect. But that is not really want I want to talk about here.

The other day a parent told me of an interesting exchange she had with her young daughter. They were riding in the car and mom apparently lost her cool over vehicular rudeness. She used language that she was not supposed to use, directed toward another motorist. Honked her horn, screamed, swore. You know, you've been there. On both ends.

Her daughter's reaction was interesting. Some kids would laugh at this spontaneous burst of naughty behavior. Others might become afraid of the strong emotions. And many might imitate the foul language. Not this budding character genius.

She said, "Ooh, mommy. I think you need a time-out."

What would you have done in this situation? Hopefully not put your head down and taken a time-out while operating a motor vehicle at high speed.

But would you have said, "I think you are right. I will take one as soon we get home"?

And then actually taken a time-out when you did get home? Well that is exactly what this mom did. Pretty impressive, I think.

Why? First of all, she was admitting that she had messed up; she had been naughty and had lost control. That is why we use time-outs for with our children, after all.

Second, she was showing great respect for her daughter by

admitting the validity of her daughter's judgment of her behavior. She was telling her daughter that she was insightful, accurate, and fair. Not a bad message. And third, she was modeling exactly the behavior she would want from her daughter, if and when the tables were turned. She was not resisting and denying and lying and fighting the need for a time-out. She was dutifully complying with the recommendation. Just what you would hope your kids would do.

Parenting for character not only takes time. Sometimes it also takes a time-out.

Volunteers for Good

VOLUNTEERING IS A LOT LIKE MOM AND APPLE PIE: PRETTY much everyone knows you are supposed to be for it. We keep hearing that the world will be a better place if we all volunteer to help others in need.

President Kennedy told us to "ask not what your country can do for you; ask what you can do for your country." And he started the Peace Corps. Others have followed suit, including a multitude of current initiatives to promote service activities among students.

Now I don't want to suggest that volunteering is universally supported. Surely there are those who choose not to heed the call, and often for reasons of selfishness. I recall once being on

> **Do good for others and live longer.**

jury duty in Milwaukee, and being interviewed by the two attorneys who were selecting the jurors for an armed robbery trial. We had spent an appreciable amount of time being questioned. A nun sat next to me praying to not be selected. I was a little surprised that she thought the use of prayer was to get you off the hook on matters of public responsibility, but I suppose it could have been difficult for her to sentence even a guilty man to life behind bars.

Then it all became moot when one prospective juror, upon being asked if he had ever been the victim of a robbery like the one before us, jumped up and yelled "Yes, and the guy who did it looked just like him!" as he pointed directly at the defendant. At this point the entire panel of prospective jurors was dismissed. As we exited, the energetic juror who got us dismissed smugly announced to us that "I knew I could get out of that one." He simply didn't want to serve. I was furious at both his lack of sense of duty and his inconsiderateness in getting all of us dismissed from our own duty.

Some folks teach that you should never volunteer for anything as a way of covering your own back and avoiding extra work and grief. Well, if you are one of those folks, do I have news for you. My wife recently told me that she had read about a new study of older adults that revealed that volunteering adds years to your life. That's *right—years* to your life.

What could speak louder to selfish people motivated primarily by self-interest? Do good for others and live longer. Why, even Madison Avenue couldn't come up with a better advertising slogan for volunteerism.

And volunteering even outstripped working for pay. You live longer volunteering than you do working. So you have two reasons to promote volunteerism for you and in your kids. If you are already a pro-social, caring, giving person, then you simply get your kids to understand, value, and engage in volunteerism because it is the right thing to do. Because it is part of good character, builds more character, and helps others.

But if you are one of those primarily self-interested types, then the second reason is just right for you. Volunteer to help others so that you will live a longer, fuller, healthier life.

Either way, the world can't lose because more of us will be out there helping others and showing good character. And if we do it, our kids will, too. You help others, help your kids develop character, and they help others as well. All just by volunteering.

Parenting 101

Anticipatory Parenting

DEALING WITH KIDS IS OFTEN A REACTIVE TASK. YOU END up reacting to what went wrong. Breaking up the fight between your four- and six-year-old boys. Punishing your teenage daughter for disrespectfully talking back to her mother. Praising your eleven-year-old son for helping his little sister with her homework. All of that is appropriate parenting, but it is decidedly incomplete.

You also need to engage in "anticipatory parenting." You may be wondering what in the world anticipatory parenting is. I don't blame you—I just made that phrase up.

Anticipatory parenting has two parts to it. First, it has to do with predicting what a kid is likely to do or what the consequences

> Life will always give them new experiences so that they can grow these skills. But while they're kids, they will be able to learn to problem-solve in anticipation if you cue them and support them.

of his or her behavior are likely to be. For instance, knowing that your three-year-old daughter is likely to run into the street to chase her kickball. Or that your eight-year-old son is likely going to try to mimic the cartoon chaos he is watching...right on top of your glass coffee table.

The second part has to do with your reactions to predictable events. When we "baby-proof" our houses, we anticipate that our toddlers are likely to open certain cabinets that are just the perfect toddler height. So we put childproof locks on them or take the dangerous materials out of them. That is safe, sensible parenting. So is not leaving our ten- and twelve-year-old sons home alone watching the World Wrestling Federation's "ultra-death smash-face megaton cage-of-torture cannibal special."

But there is more to it than that. Each of us lacks some of the skills necessary to do the right thing. It might be that we lack impulse control or good communication skills. This is especially true of children.

I remember numerous occasions when my son had a big argument with his best friend (of the moment) and they were not speaking to one another. From the big perspective (that is, from my point of view) it was clear that he and his friend were good buddies and would eventually get over it. But they didn't know how to "make up." So my wife or I prepared him for his next conversation with his friend or even prompted him to call his friend to try to make up. We would discuss what he might say and how he would react depending on how his friend responded. And it usually worked. We helped our son compensate for his less developed communication skills by anticipating what might happen and suggesting how he could reach a positive result.

We could help him overcome his nervousness about the first day of school by talking with him about what it would be like and what he could do to make it a positive experience. When we moved (twice in one year!) and he had to jump into a new school in midyear, we talked about how he could find a place to sit in the cafeteria or on the bus. We suggested how he could make new friends.

In other words, we anticipated what he might encounter and how he might prepare himself to act or react. Kids rarely have the gift of foresight to do this by themselves. While they're kids, they can learn to problem-solve in anticipation if you cue them and support them.

So if you want your child to develop good character, anticipate them doing so. To help your child avoid being offensive, you need to be defensive...in anticipation.

Gambling
with Character

YOU MAY NOT BE AWARE OF IT, BUT CHANCES ARE YOU'RE a bit of a liar and a gambler! Okay, I know those are fighting words, but before you get too angry, hear me out.

What I mean is that it's likely that at some point in your life, someone advised you, in so many words, to clean up your act for the sake of your child. Maybe you were told you shouldn't swear so much, or perhaps you were advised not to smoke cigarettes when you were pregnant, or not to hit your children. And most likely, you responded with "Hey, I was exposed to [swearing, maternal smoking, corporal punishment] and I turned out just fine!" You feel good, and, in a sense, vindicated. Much like a fencer who has managed to parry a potentially harmful thrust.

But you shouldn't. Because you've just engaged in what I call a psycho-fallacy. Instead of using logic, you used psycho-logic. And I'll give you two reasons why you shouldn't feel too smug about that mode of reasoning.

First, when someone points out a proven tendency of human behavior, it can't be disproved by a single exception. Despite the fact that a mother's smoking (or spanking, or other improper behaviors) led to no detectable harm for a particular child, that doesn't disprove overwhelming scientific evidence determining that spanking and cigarette smoke *do* tend to harm the health and development of children and fetuses.

Psychological and biological truths are rarely absolute. In fact, they are more often probabilities. In other words, if you routinely spank a child, it is *probable* that the child will psychologically suffer. If you smoke throughout pregnancy, it is *probable* that your child will suffer certain medical problems. But is it possible for a child to be unscathed? Yes, it is. But it's a gamble.

If you're the betting type, you might still be willing to bet that your potentially harmful behaviors won't harm your child. But that's a risk you have no right to take when the potential harm to your child can be devastating. If you lose your bet, your kid loses. But his loss will likely be far greater than yours.

Let's try a second approach to deflect your psycho-fallacy. How can you be certain you weren't negatively affected by your mother's smoking? After all, is it possible to ascertain what your respiratory health, height, and IQ might have been if your mother hadn't smoked when she was pregnant? And how do you know that your son wasn't negatively affected by the occasional spankings you administered? It's virtually impossible to determine whether your child might have been more pro-social and less prone to violence if you hadn't spanked him.

So, don't try to convince yourself that your child isn't vulnerable to the things that affect other children. Self-deception is one of the great human pastimes, but it's not very healthy or productive. And certainly, lying to oneself or to others is not exactly a great way to build character.

You know what is good for your child, and you know what will help him or her grow physically and emotionally strong. Chances are you also know what it takes to help develop a child's healthy character. So don't fool yourself by employing psycho-fallacy—there are certain gambles and self-deceptions that no parent should ever be willing to take, for the sake of themselves, and especially, their child.

Out of Their Minds

HOW MANY TIMES HAVE YOU SAID—OR SHOULD I SAY shouted—those words? "Are you out of your mind?" "What were you thinking?" "How *could* you?"

Well, the fact of the matter is that they probably *weren't* thinking. Or to put it another way, they were "out of their minds." Kids have a remarkable power at times of disengaging their minds from their actions.

My teenage son recently got in trouble for misbehaving on the school bus—in this case, playing with another kid's cigarette lighter. Now, if he was maliciously intending to start a fire, that would be one thing, but in this

> **Part of being responsible is being reflective. Stopping to look before you leap, and taking the time to ponder before you wander.**

instance, he simply wasn't thinking about the meaning or potential implications of his actions. He was simply doing it. When I asked him later in the principal's office, "what were you thinking?", his honest and disheartening answer was "I wasn't thinking anything." His reflective mind had momentarily disengaged in response to an exciting allure.

I told this to my friend who reported a similar incident with her teenage son. He was on the phone in the kitchen and apparently while his mind was fully focused on his conversation, his body was getting bored. So he plucked one of the knives off of the knife rack and began tapping the blade on the sink faucet right below the knife rack. Over and over again. Until he irreparably nicked the new faucet, and in the process, ruined the knife blade. When asked why he had done that, his only answer was "I wasn't thinking about it." He likely wasn't fully aware that he was even doing it.

We arrived home yesterday to a snow storm. My son immediately wanted to go to a friend's house. The favored route was cutting through two neighborhood backyards, which he did while wearing sandals, through a half-foot of snow. When I asked him later why he wore sandals, his answer was "I put them on and they were comfortable. I didn't think about having to walk through snow in the backyards."

When I discussed this column with my son, he lamented that I always write about "stupid things" he has done and not about stupid things I have done. So...

I recall joining a friend of mine, at about 12 or 13 years of age, in an open field and setting a small fire. Just for the thrill of it. We never considered that the field was constituted at the moment of dried tall grass. The fire began to spread and we barely were able to put it out. We were petrified, but had never thought about the possible consequences.

Another time, when in high school, I entered the house to find my parents hosting my aunts and uncles. Trying to show off by putting my parents down, I noticed new placemats on the counter and made some disparaging remark about what a waste of money they were. I didn't know they were a gift from my aunt and uncle. To this day, I feel the guilt and shame at having insulted and hurt them in that way. I just wasn't thinking.

Part of being responsible is being reflective. Stopping to look before you leap, and taking the time to ponder before you wander. Robert Frost did not just forge ahead on the road less taken. He took time to reflect on the meaning of that choice.

But responsibility is a characteristic of maturity, and adolescents are far from consistently mature. They have their moments, to be sure. But they also often fall far short of the mark. This is despite their unrelenting protestations that they are being treated like children and that they deserve equal status with adults. When your teenager demands adult freedoms (e.g., "Why can't teens have sex?" "What's wrong with a drink or two at a party?"), remind them of some of the times they did something unthinking, such as wearing sandals in the snow, ruining a sink, or playing with a lighter on the school bus. That may humble them.

One of the critical points here is seeing the difference between stupid, unintentional misbehavior and malicious, intentional acts of destruction. Both need to be firmly addressed, but they should not be treated the same. When a child shows some of the signs of maliciousness, cruelty, and destructiveness as an *intentional act*, especially if done repeatedly, then that is worrisome, and professional help should be sought.

But when a child simply disengages his or her brain and does something stupid that he or she knows later is wrong—but didn't even consider at the moment—then different consequences are necessary. You will reach different conclusions about the child, and that this is an act of immaturity, not of immorality.

Kids will be kids, but we don't want them to *always* be kids. So we need to help them develop maturity, along with morality. To this end, model reflective thinking for them, and prompt them to consider the consequences and meaning of their actions. Talk to them about how they screwed up by not doing so, and levy consequences for having screwed up. But don't label them as evil for being out of their minds.

It's a kid thing. There is even some research by Harvard psychologist Kurt Fisher and others that suggests that between the ages of 18–20 there may be a spurt in brain growth that directly supports the development of mature, reflective thinking capacities and capabilities. This is not an all-or-none issue, however; it is a matter of degree.

So understand it, and differentiate it from true malicious intentionality. Be patient, and work to minimize it by promoting responsible, reflective thought.

Parental Faith

THIS COLUMN IS ABOUT FAITH, BUT PROBABLY NOT THE kind you are thinking about. I am not writing here about religious faith, rather, I am writing about faith in the value of your parenting.

Think of parenting as an investment. You are investing in the adult nature of your child. By parenting effectively and wisely, you are investing in the likelihood that your child will ultimately develop into a responsible, caring, and fair adult.

Notice, however, that I said "likelihood." Not certainty, and not guarantee. Your child did not come with a warranty or a money-back guarantee. Therefore, because there is no absolute guarantee that your best parenting efforts will pay off exactly as you had intended, we need to consider the matter of faith.

Furthermore, to make all of this even more complex, as my colleague Dr. B.R. Rhoads (currently principal of Tillman Elementary School in the Kirkwood School District) has said, "Kids do not develop in straight lines." No smooth rides here, but bumps galore!

And that bumpy road is a long one. One needs faith to sustain oneself when traveling a long and bumpy road. Every parent has and will lament that they have failed, somewhere along that road. Their kids will misbehave at school, be caught bullying another child, steal something from a store, get in a fight, be cruel to a friend, and so on. As a result, you will wonder how you failed, and you may assume your child is on a trajectory for failure. Adolescence is a classic time for such self-doubts, but it happens throughout childhood.

I remember early in my relationship with my wife (way before she was my wife) when she broke up with me "for good." I was devastated. I was ultimately consoled by something one of my married friends told me. He informed me that, while dating, he and his wife had broken up "for good" many times.

Ironically, they are now divorced, and my wife and I just celebrated our thirtieth anniversary. And thinking about my crippling grief at that early break-up and looking back over our three decades together, I can honestly say that I probably overreacted.

In one way, I really did overreact. I believed that what was happening at the moment was what would happen forever. I didn't have faith in our love and our ability to weather the storm, just as we often don't have faith in our good parenting behaviors and their ultimate effects on our children. Those behaviors are investments in their future and development, and we need to maintain a strong faith that we can only do our best and that our best will likely pay off in the long run.

> **"Kids do not develop in straight lines."**

It may not seem that way when we parents are being treated like a mutant sub-species, or when kids reject personal hygiene as a form of cultural oppression. The trick is to see beyond where they are now to where we hope they will be someday. One useful device is to talk to parents whose kids once walked where yours walk now, and find out that those kids are now making it—and are doing just fine.

The ultimate goal, after all, is to guide your kids to be adults of character. When I worked at the U.S. Air Force Academy's Center for Character Development, I often noted that their true goal was not to graduate cadets of character, but to supply the U.S. Air Force with adult officers of character. The true measure of their success, in other words, was not the behavior of 20- or 21-year-old seniors at the academy, but the behavior of those same folks in their mid-twenties and beyond as commissioned officers in the U.S. Air Force.

The same is true of our kids. Certainly we want them to act with character as youth. But most important, we want them to be adults of character. So we have to see beyond the momentary misbehavior of our kids (and I am not talking about chronic misbehavior, nor serious misbehavior) to the adults they will become someday.

And that takes faith, a long-range perspective, perseverance, and an understanding about how kids grow and what parents do that affects them.

Raising the Bar

WHEN SOMEONE ASKS IF YOU ARE "EXPECTING," USUALLY it means "are you pregnant?" But it can have a different meaning, also concerning children: do you have expectations for your kids? Do you have goals for them? What do you expect of them?

There are many ingredients necessary for humans to flourish, such as love and a sense of control. Another is having goals and dreams to which one can aspire. Kids need goals and expectations.

We fail our kids if we don't expect a lot from them. Bill Damon wrote a book called *Greater Expectations*, in which he criticized American society for continually lowering the bar for children. We expect too little of them, and they deliver precisely what we expect— very little. Their academic achievement is lower than it could be. And worse, their social responsibility and moral conduct are less than they should be. Because we don't expect enough of them.

A recent middle school study by Kathryn Wentzel in the journal *Child Development* focused on whether teachers' impact on kids is similar to parents' impact on kids. One of the issues she explored was that of teachers having high expectations for their middle school students. She found that teachers with high expectations had students who had more pro-social motives and pro-social behavior, less irresponsible behavior, and higher grades in school. Those are pretty impressive findings.

This finding parallels what research tells us about parents who set high expectations for their kids. Such kids tend to flourish socially, ethically, and intellectually.

Of course, we need to understand that setting absurdly high expectations won't accomplish all these good things. In fact, it can cause more harm than good. Also, setting high expectations but not providing support or encouragement doesn't work well. You have to be instrumental in kids' lives by supporting them in their struggles and efforts.

You also have to pay attention to not only their strivings, but their outcomes. Focus on positive encouragement, and try to avoid criticism and negative feedback. The Wentzel study also found that the use of negative feedback by middle school teachers was harmful to kids' development.

> **We fail our kids if we don't expect a lot from them.**

Kids are like potted plants— they grow to fill their pots. And your expectations are their pots. If the expectations are bigger, they will grow to meet them. If the expectations are small, they will be stunted. But a rose will not grow to be a redwood. And neither will it flourish without support and nutrition.

Kids need expectations and they need them from parents, from teachers, and from the rest of society. Those expectations need to be set high, set clear, supported, and monitored. And that is one of the roots of character.

Now or Later

I AM BASICALLY A PROCRASTINATOR. I LIKE TO PUT THINGS off, if I can, and some things I put off forever. But some things— like being good—cannot be delayed for long.

There are times when you miss the opportunity to do something that is right. Sometimes because you are too lazy to put in the effort, or because you accidentally missed the chance or simply made the wrong choice. But in all cases, it is important to take the time and make the effort to make the situation right.

I just returned from a visit to another city where a colleague took me to lunch in the new faculty cafeteria at his university. He went through a complicated procedure to figure out how to charge the lunch to his account. The waitress was very helpful in working through this task. After lunch, he realized that he didn't know if the procedure included a tip for the waitress. But we quickly agreed that he should return the next week and belatedly give the waitress a tip. I realized that this was not only going to make the situation right, but probably would have a much more powerful and positive impact on the waitress than if he had given the tip to her right away. Because it meant he thought enough of her to go the extra mile for her.

The other day my father called and told me he realized he had unfairly and unnecessarily reprimanded my niece and nephew (his grandchildren) when they had visited his house. They had taken some candy from the cupboard, and he had yelled at them for taking it without permission. But he realized that he had overreacted and already had a plan to bring them candy the next time he saw them as a form of apology. I suspect that will make a great and positive impression upon them. It models right thinking and right behavior.

Kids not only need to learn the right thing, but they need to learn how to act when they don't do the right thing. None of us are perfect and we all will periodically stumble. So the question is not if we will stumble, nor even when, but rather *how* we will respond when we inevitably do.

Kids need to see adults failing (and we all provide ample opportunity for this), but even more important, they need to see adults admitting their mistakes and putting in the extra effort to make it right.

Years ago, I had the opportunity to live in Europe for a year. During this time, we visited Spain and went out to dinner one night at a pub. It was busy and the apparent routine was to order your food at the counter, take it outside to a table to eat, and when you were finished, to come inside and pay. Well, in the chaos and because we were used to paying in advance for self-service food, we ordered, ate, and left without paying. We walked back to our hotel, and got undressed and ready for bed. Then I realized what had happened.

> **Kids not only need to learn the right thing, but they need to learn how to act when they don't do the right thing.**

I also realized that no one would ever know or find us, and it was very tempting to simply forget about it. But I got dressed, walked all the way back to the pub, worked my way through the crowd, and in very broken Spanish explained and paid. To impart a lesson to my son, who was then eight years old, I told him about what I had done, and why I went back.

Kids don't need parents who are perfect. But they do need parents who do the right thing, if not now, then later.

Parenting
and School

Who Cares About School?

WHEN JULIE ANDREWS SANG ABOUT "A FEW OF HER favorite things," she didn't mention school. This is not surprising. School wouldn't be most kids' first choice for how to spend a large chunk of their waking hours.

I remember a rather startling scene from my first few minutes in school. Probably like most of my peers, I had arrived at nursery school with great fear and trepidation on my first day. One of my classmates was a bit more honest and direct than most of us in expressing his feelings about having his mother abandon him to a room full of strangers. He was standing on his hands with his feet kicking against the door and screaming at the top of his lungs, while objects poured from his pockets. He certainly got my attention (and that of everyone within earshot—probably within three or four miles). It was an Olympic-caliber performance.

School is strong stuff, and it can be scary or boring. And kids' emotional reactions to school will have an effect on both how well they do and how they develop. Recent findings suggest that attachment to school helps keep kids out of trouble. Those who feel positively attached to school, their classes, and teachers are less likely to engage in risky behaviors such as substance use and delinquency. This alone is reason enough to want to make schools less boring and unfriendly. We spend nearly half a trillion dollars a year on education, and most kids still find school boring and uninspiring. Shouldn't we try to make schools more user-friendly?

In fact, our schools, especially our high schools, are perhaps the least evolved institutions we have. Think about it: Just how different is the structure of school today from when you were a kid? And did you enjoy going to school as a kid? Probably not.

Character educators have come to discover that their effectiveness depends upon whether kids see their schools as "caring communities." If they see the school as a place where people care about each other—and especially about them—they are more likely to care about others. Kids also become more likely to support democratic values, to avoid drugs and other risky behaviors, to want to do well in school, and to get better grades.

So if we want to keep kids from losing their cool and their character, we need to help them bond to school. Schools need to be more child-friendly places, so kids learn to see their schools as places where people care about them.

But this isn't the school's responsibility alone. Parents need to work hard to develop and support a "school ethic." How? By becoming involved in their kids' education. They need to monitor and help with homework. They need to ask kids about their day at school (even if the answer is always "I dunno"). Parents, make a habit of asking about school as soon as kids get home, and then again during meal time. Parents should volunteer to help at school. They need to read messages from the principal and teacher and to promptly respond. They should tell kids stories about their own happy experiences and adventures at school.

Schools cannot merely be holding tanks for our youth. Kids need to want to attend school and to enjoy their experiences. Then they can confidently learn to stand on their own two feet, rather than hysterically on their hands.

"Homework" Is Not a Four-Letter Word

HOMEWORK IS GETTING A BAD RAP. IT NEEDS A GOOD public relations makeover. Kids detest it, because it robs them of what they see as their sacred right to stare at a TV or computer screen for hours on end, or chat with their friends on the phone. Parents hate it, because they can't figure it out ("Mom, what's a hypotenuse?" "What does iambic pentameter mean?" "Where are the Isles of Langerhans?"). And teachers have to devise it, assign it, and grade it. It can look like a lose-lose situation.

It is time for someone to come to the defense of the much maligned concept of homework. Oh, I know what you are thinking: "That's obvious. It helps kids practice and learn their school work." Kind of an extension of the school day. And you are right. But that is not what I am getting at; this is a column

> **Kids learn that families help each other, even with difficult or boring tasks. They also learn that their schoolwork and homework is important to their family. But most important, homework done this way supports bonding with parents.**

about character development, not learning. There are hidden virtues to homework that you may not have considered, so read on.

Psychologists and educators have discovered that when parents are involved in their kids' homework, kids develop in a more healthy direction. That doesn't mean parents *doing* kids' homework for them. We all remember the kid whose model of Fort Sumter looked like Frank Lloyd Wright designed it and a team of medieval artisans crafted it from trees nurtured by cloistered monks, because his dad and uncle (who just happen to be architects) built it. Or the kid whose science project looked suspiciously like what his dad did in his laboratory at work. No, what we are referring to instead are parents who monitor kids' homework and support them in effectively completing it.

Such parents care how their kids learn, and therefore whether and how they complete their homework. And they are there as a safety net when kids stumble. They offer critical pieces of advice ("I wonder if there is anything in your social studies book about that") or help with sub-tasks ("What if you just add the ones column first? How much would that be?"). And they check the work and give feedback ("Now, what kinds of words are supposed to start with capital letters? Do you see any that you may have missed?").

Parents model caring and nurturing by doing this. Kids learn that families help each other, even with difficult or boring tasks. They also learn that their schoolwork and homework is important to their family. But most important, homework done this way supports bonding with parents, perhaps the single most important ingredient in healthy character development.

The Child Development Project, generally regarded as one of the most comprehensive and effective character development programs in the field, has a special homework program called *Homeside Activities* (see *Homeside Activities Books* for grades 1–5 on their website: www.devstu.org). These are homework assignments designed specifically to be done with one's family.

Not only do such assignments serve all the goods described above, but they have the added feature of getting parents involved in their kids' schools. And teachers and principals find that this makes their schools much better places for kids to develop healthy character.

Working Together

EVER HEAR OF THE FINGER POINTING GAME? I SEE IT constantly played in my line of work. You probably see a different version in yours.

Here are the game rules: First, you need two or more people. Second, you need a problem (if you are a normal human being, you probably have plenty of these on hand). Third, you need a set of categories into which people can be divided. In my work, parents and teachers work perfectly for this game.

Now you are ready to play. Either roll dice to decide who plays first or simply let nature takes its course. Once the problem is identified, all players point their fingers at someone from a different group. For example, the teachers point at the parents and the parents point at the teachers. Pointing is the equivalent of assigning blame for a problem. The only weakness in this game is that there is rarely a winner. More than likely, all players end up being losers. And the biggest losers tend to be the children involved.

When specific children or an entire school or class has a problem (e.g., Nancy is not learning to read; Dion has been sleeping through first period; Sasha was caught cheating on a test; Mrs. Green's class got rowdy and ended up breaking something), teachers tend to blame parents ("They are not raising their kids well") and parents blame teachers ("They don't know how to teach and manage the kids in their classrooms").

There are some obvious problems with this game. First, parents and teachers end up being adversaries rather than accomplices. Second, kids' problems are not adequately addressed. Third, adults are modeling for children undesirable behavior with their poor conflict-resolution strategies and antagonistic attitudes toward other adults.

Kids need as many adults and institutions as they can get, all working for their best interests. The more, the merrier. And the more, the better the odds that a child will develop good character.

On September 11, 2001, schools, like the rest of the nation, were in turmoil. Principals and teachers weren't exactly sure what was the best thing to do to serve the children's best interests. Responses varied widely, because it was hard to know what the best course of action should be. Should we have discussions? Should we let them watch the gripping, terrifying television images and unfolding news in the classroom? At what age was it appropriate?

Some teachers told me that they encountered a crisis on September 13. Why that day? Well, some children came to school on the twelfth knowing what had happened the day before, and others had been sheltered by their parents from the knowledge of the terrorist attacks. The latter kids were then exposed to some version of the events, either in the classroom in an organized fashion from their teacher, or from their peers on the bus and playground. Parents then called on the thirteenth to complain that their hard work at sheltering their kids was undone by teachers and schools. And the finger-pointing game began anew.

It seems to me that all parties were put in a difficult situation, so conflict was likely. But well-intentioned adults should recognize that the kids have to come first. Teachers need to understand that parents are fearful for and protective of their children—and those protective parents may have wanted a little more time to decide how to discuss it at home. Parents need to appreciate that teachers are doing the best they can, and they also need to understand that it's close to impossible for their kids to attend a school with hundreds of children and to not learn about the magnitude of the acts and the ensuing tragedies and losses of so many people, for so many families.

But kids are serious business. So teachers and parents need to stop playing games, especially the finger-pointing game. Use those fingers to point the way to good character instead—by cooperating.

Peers and
Culture

The Peers from Hell

MOST PARENTS HAVE THE SAME NIGHTMARE: THEY'RE afraid that all those years of building their child's character will be wasted, once adolescent peers get their evil hands on their kid. The nightmare goes something like this:

Parents pour love, dedication, and wisdom into raising a kid with empathy, honesty, responsibility, and all those good character traits. For about a dozen years, their work pays off as others remark on their "good kid." Then on the kid's thirteenth birthday, he or she looks lovingly at those same parents and announces, "Mom, Dad, thank you

> **The healthiest adolescents have positive relationships with both parents and peers.**

so very much. For the past thirteen years you have cared for me, sacrificed for me, taught me right from wrong. You have been my anchor in the storm of childhood. And I want you to know how appreciative I am. But...now you are excess baggage. because now I have...peers!"

And, as if on cue, up rides a wild gang of teen Hell's Angels, with Steppenwolf's "Born to Be Wild" blaring in the background. Your darling child puts on a leather jacket with Satanic emblems, hops on the back of one of the bikes, spits into the dust, and, cackling and cursing at your neighbors, rides off into the sunset never to be seen again, to live a life of evil and perversion. Chalk up another victory for those nasty adolescent peers.

Fortunately, this is not even close to what really happens. First of all, the biggest influence on a kid's character is early parenting. A kid who is nurtured and loved in infancy, as a toddler, and during the preschool years is not likely to develop poor character. Certainly, there are no guarantees (your child didn't come with a warranty, as you know), but research tells us that positive emotional bonding in infancy and supportive guidance in preschool, for example, lead to many positive character traits in childhood and beyond.

Also, earlier experiences are more powerful than later ones, in general. Therefore, what happens in adolescence will have less impact than what happens earlier. But please note: this is not 100 percent guaranteed. All times in the lifespan make a difference; it is just a matter of how much of a difference they make. And remember, traumatic events can be very influential at any time.

Furthermore, parents have the greatest influence on important values even in adolescence. Adolescents' moral, religious, and political values have much more to do with their parents' values than with their peers'. Peers usually affect less important values—those that have to do with modern culture (what brand of clothing to wear or what types of music they like and listen to) or peer spheres of life (how to ask someone out on a date, which teacher to ask for a postponement of an assignment, or how to impress the varsity football coach).

Life is not a winner-take-all game. Kids with more attachment to peers don't have less attachment to parents. The healthiest adolescents have positive relationships with both parents and peers. Teens without friends are a worry. In fact, peer relations can even be therapeutic, and can help kids to solve many of their problems. Clearly, parents don't need to keep a friendship ledger worrying that "one more friend means we're history!"

Parents don't need to fear their adolescent's peers, or worry that their fourth-grader will be snatched from their tender care by evil teens. Certainly, there are dangers out there and many of them come from troubled adolescents. But such adolescents are in the minority despite what some may have you believe. The good work that you do as a parent will help ensure your kid's goodness. It will also protect him from those who would lead him astray, and it will help lead him toward healthy peer relationships.

Clothes, Conversations, and Character

VIVIDLY RECALL TWO INCIDENTS FROM MY CHILDHOOD
that revolved around my clothing. The first occurred during my
late teens, when I was home on vacation from college. It was the late
1960s, a time of unique teen style sometimes referred to as "military-
surplus-dumpster chic." Of course, I followed the dress code mantra
common to my age group.

One evening, my family was preparing to go to a restaurant for
dinner. After giving careful consideration to clothing options, I
chose a threadbare pair of jeans I had painstakingly decorated with
a variety of hand-sewn patches covering worn spots at the knees, seat,
and crotch. I liked the jeans and I was proud of what I had
contributed to their splendor. So I was startled by the intensity of my
father's objections to them.

It would be an understatement to say that he went ballistic. To this
day, I all too vividly recall the yelling, threatening, and tears that
followed. All over a pair of worn jeans and what I thought were some
nifty-looking patches.

Dad took plenty of time to make it clear that it was nothing less
than a cardinal sin to go to a respectable restaurant dressed like a
derelict. But I, being of superior adolescent stock, couldn't
understand what he was fussing about and held my ground. The
upshot was that dinner was spoiled for me, for dad, and for everyone
else in the family. More surprising is the fact that the incident was so

powerful that everyone in the family remembers it to this day—more than thirty years later.

The second incident, which occurred ten or fifteen years later, was somewhat less dramatic, but I'll include it here because it effectively serves my point. My wife and I were visiting with my parents, and again we were about to go out for dinner. And again there was an argument about how inappropriate it was to go to a restaurant wearing seedy-looking jeans. And once again there was yelling and digging in of heels. But there was a difference this time: It was my father, now in his 60s and wearing worn jeans, who refused to change into something more respectable. And it was my mother who was demanding that he do so.

I doubt that there are many families that have not had arguments over a child's appearance—whether it had to do with clothing, hairstyle, jewelry, make-up, or something else. (My hair—at least when I used to have hair—was an ongoing source of arguments with my father. And it already is with my son.)

There are several interesting facets here. Most obviously, of course, is the fact that we are dealing with disagreements that involve both taste and values. I don't want my son piercing his nose or tattooing his neck. I not only think it looks terrible, but I also don't believe in body modification or mutilation for the sake of ornamentation. After all, if we were meant to hang ornaments from our body, I believe we would have been born pre-drilled.

The challenge here lies in the fact that we parents have to find ways to deal with parent/child disagreements in productive rather than destructive ways, as we work to build their character. It's easy to put one's foot down and hold firm. And sometime it's easier to surrender. However, negotiation is most often better than either of those options.

If your child is planning to do something to her body that's irreversible or harmful, then it is your parental obligation to speak up. Do your homework, and discuss the health issues that may be at stake. If you do so based on good judgment, chances are your child will come to realize the wisdom of your decision. However, if you are dealing with something that you merely find aesthetically displeasing (such as my patchwork jeans, my father's faded jeans, or my son's spiked hair, for example), then it's best that you express your opinion (civilly, please)—and live with it. And if you feel you can't live with it, then learn to.

Why? Because self-expression is a critical part of becoming a whole person. It is a part of growing up that is central to normal adolescent development and it begins well before the teen years. Kids need leeway in deciding their appearance, slang expressions, and behavior patterns. Little things, such as saying "dude" incessantly, wearing a special necklace or ring, decorating their backpacks, or hanging a particular poster on a bedroom door are ways of saying *"I am someone."* And feeling as though you are someone is a building block in the development of character. Socrates, Abraham Lincoln, Mahatma Gandhi, Rev. Martin Luther King, Jr., and Mother Teresa could not have done the great and moral things they did if they hadn't felt confident in following personal convictions. And that begins with establishing an identity—being someone.

There is an important difference between matters of taste and matters of right and wrong, however, and it is of utmost importance that we identify and treat each accordingly. Matters of taste can, and should, be tolerated. Let your child wear her hair looking like a subtropical bird after a rainstorm. Let your son patch his jeans, even if they don't need it, in order to express himself. And let your father wear his favorite pair of faded jeans. That's all okay. But when the issue has to do with health, harm to self or others, or offending the general public (with obscenities, symbols of hatred, etc.), then we're talking about the domain of morality and about right and wrong. And in those instances, parents need to take quick and decisive action.

We must teach our children about right and wrong and respect for others. In order to accomplish this, we must be fair, we must be consistent, and we must clearly express our values. Most important, we parents must model good behavior so that our children will know it's not just something we talk about, but something we actually do, even when it isn't easy.

Good Sports

ONCE UPON A TIME, THERE WAS A LAND WHERE THE youth engaged in sporting activities. They threw, kicked, and caught balls, ran, jumped, swam, and engaged in many other such sports. Sometimes they competed, sometimes they trained, and sometimes they simply played. And all of this activity was done because it helped promote the character of the youth of this land.

All was well, until the adults became interested in other aspects of the play of the youth. They became spectators at youth sports activities, and began to press their children to do better at these games. They invested their time and money and emotional energy into youth sports, and began to live vicariously through their children's exploits. Some of them even began to bet on the outcomes of youth competition. Those adults who led youth sports became corrupted. They cut corners, pushed youth too hard, and eventually took the joy out of youth sports. Worse yet, they drained the character out of it, too.

Somehow, what began as a means of promoting positive youth character became a means to promote deceit, ugly competition, distorted self-concepts, emotional pain, and short-term and even chronic physical damage to the children.

Nice fairy tale, huh? Not exactly. As the old Walt Kelly line (paraphrasing Oliver Perry) says, "We have met the Enemy, and they is US!"

We have taken what was once explicitly designed as a means to contribute to the character development of our youth, and turned it into an ugly and anti-child phenomenon. And parents are the worst culprits. Just watch them at youth sports events—they are rabid: screaming invectives at the coaches, officials, the other parents, and even the children themselves. If, like me, you have ever refereed at such an event, you have probably considered surrendering your membership card to the adult human race.

And it is not just the parents that are spectators. The vast majority of youth volunteer coaches are parents. And many of them are falling far short of the mark when it comes to promoting the potential positive outcomes of youth sports, like good-sportsmanship, cooperation, graciousness in winning as well as losing, and respect for the game.

Now, if this were truly a fairy tale, there would be a hero about to arrive on the scene to save the day. Well, it is not a fairy tale, but help is on the way.

The popular character education organization, Character Counts!, began a positive youth sports initiative entitled *Pursuing Victory with Honor* (www.charactercounts.org). Dr. Jeffrey Beedy, a forerunner in this field, has established a summer youth camp to promote character through positive sports based on his book *Sports P.L.U.S.* (www.sportsplus.org), and numerous other books about positive youth sports are now available also. One that specifically targets how parents can help clean up youth sports and promote character is *It's Just a Game* by Darrell Burnett. There are a multitude of national and local organizations that are trying to promote the positive character effects of youth sports (like the American Youth Soccer Organization, the Positive Coaching Alliance, and the National Association for Sport and Physical Education).

These are just some of the resources to help you think more deeply about the effect sports can have on your child's character, and the effect your proper involvement in your kid's sports can have, as well. Model good sportsmanship, encourage good character over winning at all costs, and join organizations that are trying to make a difference.

Raising Potatoes

TR from Arizona writes: "My seventeen-year-old son loves his computer so much, he spends virtually every waking hour on it. I don't think that is healthy. Should I be concerned?"

MOVE OVER IDAHO! IT SEEMS THAT THE REST OF AMERICA is also raising potatoes. Couch potatoes, that is.

Parents frequently lament the time their couch potato kids spend staring at a TV screen or computer monitor. To be perfectly honest, this is a point of contention between me and my fourteen-year-old son as well.

Clearly, American kids watch too much television, spend too much time on the computer and telephone, eat unwisely and too much, and get too little physical exercise. As my friend Tom Lickona, author of *Raising Good Children*, once said, "Every hour spent in front of the television is an hour that could have been spent doing something productive."

Nonetheless, it is important to determine the facts before jumping to conclusions about how kids spend their time. Parents should first find out exactly how much time their kids really spend staring at a TV or computer screen. Often, it is less than they thought—but more than their kids admit. (And what are they watching on TV? Is it really mindless, or is it perhaps something educational?)

A good exercise is to have each child guesstimate how much time he or she *thinks* is spent on these activities. Next, ask them each to keep a log to determine the *actual* time spent. Then, if a child is found to be living an unhealthy lifestyle, change is warranted, for the sake of both the child's health and character.

But there is yet another issue here. When parents tell me their kids spend too much time doing something, I have to ask why they let them do it. Having access to a computer is not the eleventh commandment nor is it listed in the Bill of Rights (although my son would probably argue that it should be).

What would those same parents do if, rather than becoming stuck on the computer, their kid were stuck on pornography or marijuana or engaged in repeated acts of vandalism?

If a child's chosen activity isn't healthy, then it's the parents' job to intervene. Parents are responsible for the habits their children develop. Habits are building blocks for character, and good habits typically lead to positive character.

My son is a rather reluctant reader, so we set up a system whereby he earns time on the computer by reading. Every minute reading earns two minutes of computer time.

> **If a child's chosen activity isn't healthy, then it's the parents' job to intervene. Parents are responsible for the habits their children develop; these habits are building blocks for character.**

Don't get me wrong—the system is not flawless and his compliance did not come easily. But our new policy seems to have both increased his reading time and reduced his computer time. The computer was the "default option" before: Momentarily bored? Why then, turn the computer on.

Let me quote Tom Lickona once more: "The TV should be like every other appliance in the house: its normal state should be 'off.' And you should have a reason to turn it on. You don't leave the microwave running just in case you want to heat something up later on, do you?"

Kids need parents to provide structure to their lives in order to help them make good choices and develop good habits, and to help them to become good people—not good potatoes.

Sex, Drugs, and Rock 'n' Roll

Part I—Sex

I CAME OF AGE IN THE 1960S AND FOUND MYSELF IN THE ERA of sex, drugs, and rock 'n' roll. Some of you may recall that such things comprised the mantra of that particular generation. Now, I look back on those days from the weary, nearsighted eyes of a middle-aged man. Things sure do look different from here.

I want to talk about my reflections on these topics, particularly as they relate to parenting for character. I'll do this in three parts—the first is about children and sex, and the part this element plays in a child's character development.

> **Research shows that when we discuss sex with our children, most of us don't know what we're talking about.**

I want to begin by saying that sex is not a bad thing; in fact, it's a good thing. Let's put that on the table right now. Of course, I don't mean to suggest that sex anywhere with anyone at any time is good; not by a long shot. (Note: I'm probably more liberal than some and more conservative than others, so don't expect to agree with everything I have to say on this controversial topic.)

So that you will have a better understanding of how I came to form my point of view, it might be important for you to know that I spent twenty years working at a Jesuit university where the Jesuit fathers had chosen to forgo sex altogether. And I got along with them just fine. So I think you and I can still be friends after you've read this column.

As I said, sex is good. The problem is that sex is not good for young children or for adolescents. Now, you may believe that premarital sex is wrong or maybe you believe it's acceptable under certain circumstances. Regardless, you probably agree that adolescents shouldn't be free to have sex with whomever they choose whenever they feel like it. Which, for teenage boys, is anytime they're conscious and frequently when they're not.

When compared with other industrialized nations, America is recognized as being a pretty uptight society when it comes to sex. Because of our puritanical heritage, most of us tend to find it difficult to talk to our children about sex. To make matters worse, research shows that when we discuss sex with our children, most of us don't know what we're talking about.

But we must talk to our children. Regardless of our concerns, our children will someday reach puberty and the vast majority will eventually choose to have sex. So it's essential that children understand what it is all about.

Typically, children ask parents questions they don't know, are difficult to answer, or produce anxiety about the subject. And when they do ask such questions, parents often find themselves in a psychological crisis.

So here's what I suggest: Answer the question. That is providing, of course, that you know the answer. If you don't, then do your homework and promise to find it. There are a multitude of books for adults to explain sex to their children and for adolescents to read that are written especially for them. Be sure to explain the answer in language the child can understand. Try "Women can start a baby growing once a month" and not "Lunar cycles of hormonal changes in the female reproductive system potentiate conception once every two fortnights." And don't answer more than the child is really asking. Remember the old joke about the child who asked, "Where did I come from?" to which mom stuttered through a painful explanation of sex and reproduction. The child, looking confused, then said in bewilderment, "Gee, I thought I came from Memorial Hospital."

Own up to your discomfort if you're having trouble answering your child's questions. For example, you might say, "You know, it's silly but I wasn't raised in such a way as to be able to talk about sex easily. There's nothing wrong with it, but grandma and grandpa never taught me how to do it well. You've asked a really good question, so I'm going to do my best to try to answer it, even if I'm not very good at doing so." That way, you've modeled honesty. You've also relieved the child of any guilt he or she might feel from having asked a tough question.

And perhaps most important, you've taught him that talking about sex isn't bad. See? Even sex can be part of effective parenting for character.

Part II—Drugs

THIS IS PART TWO OF A THREE-PART SERIES OF ARTICLES IN which I revisit "Sex, Drugs, and Rock 'n' Roll," the mantra of my adolescence. In the last column I discussed how to build character in children when talking about sex. Now it's on to drugs.

Most parents dread the possibility of having their kids become involved with drugs. Worse, recent research suggests that the fear is well justified. According to the *Monitoring the Future* study (www.monitoringthefuture.org), more than half of twelfth-graders in the U.S. have used an illegal drug at least once. Although that figure is the highest it has been since 1987, it doesn't include alcohol, which has been used by four out of every five high school seniors, or cigarettes, used by nearly two out of three seniors. Even more frightening is the number of children who have used drugs within the last 30 days: one in four for illegal drugs, one in three for cigarettes, and one in two for alcohol.

Where does parenting for character come into play in all this? Two of the biggest contributors to kids becoming involved with drugs are parents who use drugs themselves and parents who voice pro-drug attitudes and sentiments. If a kid has parents who smoke marijuana or use cocaine then, unsurprisingly, that kid is considerably more likely to use drugs. And if parents joke about drug use, talk about how much fun they are, argue that drugs aren't dangerous, or condone their use by others, then again, their children are more likely to become involved with drugs.

Fortunately, there are things parents can do to diminish their kids' likelihood of using drugs. Parents can buffer them against the temptation of drug use by promoting religion and spirituality in the family, by developing close and loving relationships with their kids, by staying actively involved in their kids' lives, and by expecting their kids to succeed in school, and life in general. It's also critical to keep the lines of communication open.

Talk to your child about drugs and life and worries and pressures and temptations. But also make sure you *listen* to what your child has to say on these issues, because kids often try to conceal personal concerns. When your daughter says, "I'm worried that Jane may start using drugs because kids keep pressuring her," discuss her concern for Jane, but be certain to also ask your daughter if she too is worried about using drugs herself, and whether she also feels such pressures. Having learned that you remained calm while discussing Jane's problem, your daughter may feel comfortable enough to deal with personal issues that were at the heart of the discussion.

> **Make sure you *listen* to what your child has to say on these issues, because kids often try to conceal personal concerns.**

We must remember that just because our own lives are more complicated and pressure-laden than our children's, they are certainly not immune to feeling pressure. It's their experiences that matter more than our perception of their experiences. In other words, it's all about how it seems and feels to them.

Trying to turn a child's mountains into molehills doesn't work. What looks like a molehill to an adult often seems like Mt. Everest to a child. As that famous philosopher, Jiminy Cricket, once said, "Let your conscience be your guide." When you're mountain climbing it's a good idea to take along a guide. Volunteer to be your children's guide in order to help them climb that mountain known as life.

Doing so will help build both your child's conscience *and* her character.

Part III—
Rock 'n' Roll

THIS IS THE LAST OF A THREE-PART SERIES OF ARTICLES ON "Sex, Drugs, and Rock 'n' Roll." In the first two columns, I explored sex and drugs and how properly dealing with them in the family can help to build a child's character. Now we turn to rock 'n' roll, still one of my great passions.

Depending upon one's point of view, rock 'n' roll—and I use the term broadly here to include all of its many facets including hip-hop, rap, classic rock, teen pop, new wave, ska, grunge, heavy metal, etc.— is either the liberating anthem of youth or an evil tool used by kids to punish their parents. Either way, it allows kids to express the deep and confusing pains of being adolescent, or it's high-decibel auditory torture specifically designed to target frazzled parental nerves.

Regardless of one's point of view, it is clear that rock 'n' roll is at the heart of many parent/child conflicts. So let's take a closer look at the issue.

Parent: "That music is too loud! How many times do I have to tell you to TURN IT DOWN?"

Child: "Whaaat?"

Parent: "Your music is garbage. And do you call that singing? It sounds more like a warthog in a meat grinder!"

Child: "Whaaat?"

Parent: "Do you realize what they're singing about? They are saying it's fun to kill people. Do you agree with that?"

Child: "Whaaaat?"

There are three very different issues here. The first, loudness, affects everyone within earshot so that needs to be negotiated. Maybe your son or daughter can agree to turn down the volume, close the door to his room, or both. Another solution might be for him to listen to his music at full volume only when you're not within range (like within the same city). It's also important to address a very real health-related concern: It has been scientifically proven that exposure to high-decibel sounds causes permanent hearing damage and in some cases, hearing loss. Therefore, perhaps your child can use headphones designed so that the sound can only reach a level that will not cause permanent damage to the child's hearing.

The second issue—whether his music is garbage or not—is a matter of aesthetics and is best left alone. If your child likes the music, fine. After all, we listened to Bob Dylan and Neil Young and neither of them will ever be mistaken for Pavarotti. And the

> **Adolescents...want to announce to the world that they have their own values, tastes and lifestyle and that theirs are different from those of their parents'. And rock 'n' roll is a great tool for proving that.**

same goes for many other widely accepted mainstream musicians. Dismissing what kids like is not good policy and should be done only when there are issues of concern that relate to moral values or potential harm. After all, you'll have enough disagreements with your child without unnecessarily adding to the list.

But the third issue—that of moral unacceptability—is an extremely important one that relates directly to character building.

As we all know, adolescents need to establish a subculture in order to show they are not like their parents. They want to announce to the world that they have their own values, tastes, and lifestyle and that theirs are different from those of their parents'. And rock 'n' roll is a great tool for proving that. It's all about rebellion against the dominant adult culture. However, one of the real challenges that today's kids face has to do with the fact that their parents grew up on rock 'n' roll as well, so the kids have to stretch all the more to make their music unique.

We have an unusual problem in our household: I like many current groups such as U2, Smashing Pumpkins, Reel Big Fish, etc., so it turns out that my son and I often enjoy the same music. And as might be expected, he has to stretch further to create disagreements over music. Luckily for him, there is rap music. Real problems arise, however, when music contains antisocial messages, messages that promote racism or sexism, or encourage self-harm.

Those who follow this column won't be surprised to hear me say that this is yet another opportunity to talk about important issues. However, be sure not to just rant. And handle the issue carefully when choosing what you want to ban from your household. First of all, take some time and actually *listen* to the music, as unpleasant a task as that may sound. Make sure to explain if and why you're bothered or offended because, believe it or not, kids are often unaware of exactly what you object to. Tell your kid what's wrong with a lyric's message. Don't overlook the band as a whole and the musicians individually and what they stand for either.

When my son was about nine, we jointly discovered a group that remains popular to this day. We both liked their music so we bought their recording. Shortly thereafter, I read an article that told how the musicians had been linked to the white supremacist movement, so I told my son what I had learned and why he could no longer play the group's music in our home.

It would be putting it mildly to say that he was unhappy about my decision. But dealing with the issue helped us explore the subject of bigotry and whether listening to such groups has the potential to affect one's values and development. One particularly interesting argument had to do with whether just listening to it might be considered less offensive than owning it. The jury's still out on that.

Parents must also be sensitive to their children's developmental level. For example, what may be appropriate for a child age fourteen might well be unacceptable for a child of nine. When my son was younger and more impressionable, I was much more vigilant about language contained in the lyrics of the music he chose. Now that he's older, I don't feel the language is quite as treacherous to his character formation. I do want to make it clear, however, that I am still concerned about music's messages and the overall effect they have on children.

Thanks to the Internet, we can deal with this quite efficiently. (I never thought I would write those words in a column about parenting for character!) When my son wants to buy a new CD I ask him to download and print the lyrics for me. Then I read them while he paces anxiously, waiting to see if I will discover some unsavory ideas. If I don't, he can buy the recording. If I do, then we discuss what the words mean and whether our family has an issue with the message.

So, don't think of today's rock 'n' roll as the devil's noise. Most of it's just fine even if we parents don't get it. In fact, at least some of it promotes acceptable values and concepts. Peter Yarrow (of Peter, Paul and Mary fame) has taught me that music is a marvelous tool for getting people to address a variety of important issues. His current project, *Don't Laugh at Me* (www.dontlaugh.org), utilizes music to fight hatred and violence in schools. And when music really is bad, that also presents an opportunity to discuss character—or the lack thereof. You're likely to find that such discussions will strengthen the relationship between you and your child.

And of course as always, all issues between parent and child need to be dealt with respectfully and responsibly, and with mutual love and care.

Skills and Virtues

Civil Power

AS WE LOOK FOR NEW SOURCES OF POWER, WE SHOULD not overlook the power of a smile. It is remarkable how much one can accomplish with a positive greeting. Or an affirmation of one's positive regard for another.

Kids are not born knowing this. They need to learn it. And it is much more complicated than simply learning a fact.

Children (or anyone for that matter) need to not only learn the fact that a positive greeting is important in human relations. They also need to value the positive impact of a smile. And they need to learn how to be civil and positive with others. There is some skill involved here as well.

> **There is real power in sincere civility. It affirms others' sense of self worth. It nurtures relationships. It builds community. And it fosters the development of character.**

When my wife was a geriatric social worker, she had an elderly client who didn't know how to look another person in the eye, greet them assertively, smile at them, or shake their hand. He was socially crippled. So she taught him these skills, practicing them with him in the privacy of the therapist-client relationship. And his world eventually changed.

I had the great privilege of spending almost a year at the United States Air Force Academy. I spent all that time immersed in a culture of civility. People routinely smile and greet total strangers. They look for opportunities to interact positively with one another, including those situations we all gloss over such as checkout lines, service visits, elevator trips, etc. I had previously scoffed at what I thought were superficial and phony acts of civility. I learned how ignorant I was.

There is real power in sincere civility. It affirms others' sense of self-worth. It nurtures relationships. It builds community. And it fosters the development of character.

So as we raise our children, we need to pay attention to smiles and handshakes and hugs and other acts of civility and friendship. And more important, we need to model such behavior for our children because they learn from observing what we do.

We need to teach the skills necessary for such behavior. I remember when my son first started going to dances. He lamented that he was constantly rejected by girls he asked to dance. Until we diagnosed his "move" and realized that he needed to see himself from the girl's perspective and simply approach a girl with a smile and a positive demeanor. Now he suffers from "Saturday Night Fever."

We need to talk to our children about how important it is to treat others in a positive manner, even if we don't particularly like them. Getting them to consider how they feel when others "dis" them or ignore them is a critical ingredient in this character education.

So smile your way to good character, and see how far you can go.

Score a Goal
for Character

EVERY NEW YEAR, MANY PEOPLE MAKE ALL SORTS OF resolutions, plans, and goals. Of course, many of them end up in the trash heap next to withered Christmas trees, broken toys, and crumpled wrapping paper.

These resolution breakers sprawl on the sofa, smoking cigarettes, drinking another beer, relentlessly changing channels, and mourning their failed plans to lose weight, exercise, eat better, or be nicer to their parents. Not a pretty picture.

> **Goal-setting is related to happiness, a sense of well-being in life, and, potentially, good character.**

But we shouldn't be completely down on them. For they have found one secret to life's success: making plans and setting goals. Goal-setting is related to happiness, a sense of well-being in life, and, potentially, good character.

The problem with these folks is that they set goals, make plans, and then fail to meet them. But at least they're on to something.

I recently heard a speech by a high school girl who won recognition for an essay she wrote about her own goals and standards. She was able to resist the temptations and peer pressure to engage in a set of dangerous behaviors (marijuana use, teen sex, etc.) by having set explicit goals for herself that helped her to follow her values and stay true to her course.

The recognition she received was part of a program in many schools called the *Laws of Life Essay Contest,* sponsored by the John Templeton Foundation (www.lawsoflife.org). It was inspired by the writings of Sir John Templeton, and it offers students the opportunity to explore and articulate in the form of a school-based essay contest some central principle by which they choose to live.

Psychologist Robert Emmons has explored the role of goals in establishing a sense of personal meaning and promoting well-being and happiness. He has found that there are three major categories of goals that lead to success in life: intimacy, spirituality, and generativity.

Intimacy involves goals for close relationships; spirituality concerns goals related to transcending the self; and generativity has to do with goals for taking care of others.

So if one sets goals, one has some purpose to life. And if one sets goals around intimacy, spirituality, and generativity, then one also tends to experience one's life as fulfilling, resulting in a sense of well-being.

Interestingly, there is research that shows that over the entire course of adulthood, making plans and being organized predicts success in the social and work aspects of life. It seems that setting goals, particularly goals for healthy relationships, service to others, and meaning in life—and planning one's life around them—actually works.

Sir John Templeton and his staff had a good idea in encouraging kids to reflect on the values that guide their lives and to set goals around them. Now it is your turn. Help your kids think about what values are important to live by, and encourage them to set goals and plans that correspond to those important life values. Then, assist them in staying on track.

Not only will you be serving their future success, but you will also be shaping character that cares about and serves others. Set good goals and you will score a goal...for your kid's character.

Promises, Promises

I HAVE PROMISED TO WRITE ONE OF THESE COLUMNS each week. I take promises very seriously; after all, they represent a commitment that others rely upon. They trust us and depend upon us, and the expectation is that when someone says "I promise," you can count on whatever they promised to really happen.

This is most obvious when someone fails to fulfill a promise—when they "let you down." Our reaction is usually pretty intense. We are angry and disappointed, and feel betrayed.

It makes sense that we need to help our kids develop an understanding of the importance of promises and a commitment to keeping them. This is a part of nurturing and helping our kids to develop good character.

So, how do we do that? First, we need to actually model promise-keeping. We should keep our promises, and expect others to keep theirs. We need to be sure that we let kids in on our promise-keeping. Unless we tell them, they simply may not be aware of promises we make and keep.

Second, we need to talk to them about the importance of promise-keeping. Read them stories about promises made, kept, or broken.

Third, discuss promises together and let them reflect on the issues, gray areas, and challenges of promise-keeping. Give them opportunities to participate in discussions. After all, promising is a complex and challenging enterprise, and it may confuse and even threaten them. How often does a kid get enticed into telling a deep dark secret ("Who do you have a crush on?") because of the promise of confidentiality ("I swear I won't tell anyone. Cross my heart and hope to die! So, c'mon, tell me. Is it Cindy?")? Then, you have the torturous decision of whether to trust the promise.

This idea of discussion is important for another reason. As kids develop, they grow in complexity regarding how they understand promises. At first, promises are not understood at all. Sometimes they are understood as being contingent upon the receiving of a promise in return, i.e., "You should keep a promise in case you need a bigger promise from that person some day," a kind of "you scratch my back, and I'll scratch yours" notion. Eventually, usually after the early elementary years, kids come to understand promises as acts of mutual trust and social bonding. Later, they understand them as social contracts—as commitments that bind people together in moral obligation.

Discussing your kids' ideas about promises will let you in on how they understand such behavior, and sometimes it will really surprise you. I remember one high school boy telling me that you shouldn't keep promises because "a kid might make you promise to steal something from a store and if you do it, he might make you do even worse stuff later." Not your standard understanding of promises, but it was his understanding, nonetheless.

Discussing the act of making and keeping promises also is a way to stretch kids' understanding and help them develop even more mature and complete ways of thinking about them. Discussion can stimulate growth and development of character.

So, think about promises and start to foster the development of responsible promise-keeping in your kids. It will help them develop good character. I promise.

The Welcome Mat

MOST PARENTS CAN'T HELP BUT WONDER ABOUT THE friends their kids drag home. It appears as though they go out of their way to find friends who you thought existed only in your worst nightmare. You know what I'm talking about here: kids who look or act weird (or both). Kids dressed in things sane people don't wear, kids with spiked hair that defies the laws of gravity, kids with eight piercings—none of which are visible outside their clothing—kids who are sullen,

> **Some of your kids' friends are so terrifying, it's likely you've contemplated banning them from your home. Don't.**

kids who use words you don't know and are afraid to look up. In fact, some of your kids' friends are so terrifying, it's likely you've contemplated banning them from your home.

Don't.

As kids work to choose and make friends, they're considering aspects that you, as an adult, often can't see or understand. In truth, many of your child's friendships will be short-lived, for if his friends are really antisocial or misguided, it's likely he will recognize that fact and jettison the friendship on his own. It's an old axiom that bad friends usually manage to wear out their welcome.

Of course, one can't wear out a welcome if he's never had one. So it's your responsibility as a parent to welcome your children's friends into your home. I don't mean to suggest that you are obliged to accept them non-judgmentally if they are really hurtful or if they engage in dangerous behaviors. After all, it's your job to do all you can to protect your children from danger. But if your kids' friends are just different, if they lack social skills, or if they're merely acting on that age-old adolescent need to shock adults, you should still make them welcome in your home.

Keep in mind that it is very important to your children that you accept their friends. Aside from the obvious, there is an often unrecognized benefit for doing so: Psychiatrist Harry Stacks Sullivan posits that an adolescent's friends often play a therapeutic role and, on occasion, can even help solve their emotional problems.

Even more important is the fact that modeling hospitality and acceptance can have an important effect on your child's character. Samuel Oliner, in his study of Christian rescuers of Jews during World War II, found that those who engaged in heroic and dangerous acts tended to come from homes in which the parents welcomed visitors, showing them both hospitality and generosity.

As I frequently tell teachers with whom I work, it may well be the kid you like the least who needs you most. In fact, it's possible that you might become the savior of a child your kid drags home by simply offering him or her acceptance.

By adapting an old African proverb, one might say it takes a village to raise a child—of character. And by taking your responsibility as a member of the village seriously, you are helping to build your child's character while simultaneously contributing to the character of their friends.

Honesty
Is the Best Policy

SOMETIMES IT SEEMS OKAY TO JUST BEND THE TRUTH A little. Like when your boss's secretary asks your opinion of her new outfit which looks like a sure-fire winner at the annual People Without Taste convention. Or when your best friend's wife asks if you agree with their investment decision to buy stock in a company specializing in eight-track tape technology. In such cases, little white lies might be justifiable. After all, sometimes the damage and hurt the truth will cause is far worse than the nick in your character's armor. That is, unless your kids are watching. Then, you should consider the potential collateral damage.

When you choose the truth-stretching option, you had at least better take the little ones aside and attempt to explain the difference between the garden variety lie and its less caustic form sometimes called the "white lie," which is sometimes told to protect from hurt. (No easy feat by the way.) In general, however, when the kids are watching—which is most of the time—honesty is the best policy for their character as well as your own.

> When the kids are watching— which is most of the time— honesty is the best policy for their character as well as your own.

I remember a situation that took place a few years ago when some friends and I took our kids to see a University of Wisconsin Badgers' game. This was back when the Badgers hadn't been doing well and tickets were generally easy to obtain on game day. With that in mind, we planned to show up and buy ours at the gate. Unfortunately, this particular game was the first sell-out, so there we were, standing in the stadium parking lot, listening to the roar of the crowd. What a disappointment!

My friend decided to take action. He approached one of the guards and launched into a far-fetched tale that he hoped would convince the attendant to admit us sans tickets. Unfazed and unaffected, the ticket taker told us to get lost. My friend led us to another gate where he tried yet another absurd story. We were sent packing again. The third time was no charm, either.

That's when I decided to put an end to this embarrassing and character-toxic modeling. I led the troops to yet another gate, deciding to try the truth for a change. I said, "Excuse me, but I hope you can help us. We brought our kids to see today's game, never suspecting it would be a sell-out. Would you consider letting us in so we can at least show our kids the stadium—and maybe find some empty seats we might use?" The guard glanced at the kids—then opened the gate and let us in. The truth can magically open gates.

As you can certainly imagine, I gloated over my triumph until everyone eventually tired of hearing about it. But more importantly, I used it as a demonstration to my son that honesty *is* the best policy. Honesty is also one of the building blocks of character. And one that parents should attempt to model to their children at all times.

Charity Begins at Home

ONE OF THE GREAT PRACTICES IN THE JUDEO-CHRISTIAN tradition from the Old Testament is *tzedakah*, or charity. As a nation, America holds a tradition of giving to needier countries and groups around the world. Individuals give to service groups that give to individuals. It is a great tradition and one we need to continue to foster by raising children to be charitable, which encompasses the character traits of caring, compassion, and generosity.

One way to do this is to involve children in charitable acts from an early age and throughout their childhood and adolescent years. If it is part of your family to be charitable, first make sure that your kids know about it. Tell them of the check you just wrote for a particular charity. Bring them along to a fundraising event and explain the purpose of the work that you care about, and why you support it. Tell the story of your involvement in helping others in need. I know of families that volunteer at a homeless shelter or soup kitchen preparing and serving meals every week. They take their children along with them because those kids learn more by participating in charitable acts than by hearing about them.

Recently, my wife was asked to volunteer at an event in which a local chapter of the National Council of Jewish Women was running a back-to-school store for needy children. Volunteers had organized donations of new clothes and school supplies from merchants, manufacturers, and others, and additional volunteers would staff the one-day giveaway.

Needy children were brought in to the "store" and a personal shopper (one of the volunteers) would take them around with a checklist (without their parents, who, if they were there, were waiting in a separate room). Each child got to pick out the items on his or her list, for example, a winter coat, a pair of shoes, a backpack, a toiletry kit, and pencils.

I suggested that my wife take along our son to help. She asked him and he agreed, somewhat reluctantly. It didn't sound as exciting as practicing bicycle tricks with his buddies, but he went.

It was a great success all around. The children who were "shopping" were enthralled and in a state of grateful awe. When our son saw that—and it was hard to miss—he began to grasp how fortunate he is. He could see how significant a pair of shoes or a new toothbrush can be to a child. And he got to experience how rewarding it can be to help someone else, as he gave advice to little girls about how attractive they looked in one coat or another. He saw their eyes sparkle and their mouths break into uncontrollable grins. He felt their joy and gratitude.

That is powerful stuff. The kind of stuff that builds character.

Teaching Forgiving

EVER NOTICE THAT SOME PEOPLE APOLOGIZE FOR everything? I truly hope that I haven't offended you or made you uncomfortable if you are one of those incessantly apologetic folks. And I am sorry if this was just so obvious that it wasn't worth wasting your time reading it. I just thought perhaps you might find it interesting, but I sincerely regret any annoyance this column might be causing you.

Get the picture?

So you might conclude that apologizing is a social blight.

Sometimes. But usually it is well-received and socially productive. I don't want to belabor this point, as I have discussed apologizing and owning up to one's foibles in a previous column. Rather I would like to focus on how one responds to apologies. Forgiveness.

Recently, my son deeply angered one of his friends by his inappropriate behavior. His friend

> **Parents need to teach their children that good character entails not only doing the right thing up front, but also doing the right thing in the aftermath of wrong behavior, by oneself or by others... And they need to teach their kids how to accept apologies and how to forgive others.**

had a legitimate gripe. My son had messed up. But I was impressed by my son's subsequent actions. He not only messed up, he 'fessed up. He owned up to the fact that he had erred and sincerely apologized to his friend. Ever since he was a small child, we have taught him not to hold grudges and to apologize sincerely when you are wrong.

In other words, we had taught him the importance of mending social fences. Research has shown that popular children tend to have good relationship repairing skills. They know how to get beyond the inevitable conflicts of childhood and any other time in the life-span, for that matter; there is similar research on successful marriages, for instance.

The problem in the case of my son and his friend is that his friend chose to hold on to his anger. He refused to accept the apology, and he refused to speak to or spend time with my son. This was especially problematic as they had mutual friends. It got to the point of absurdity, of pouting, of truly socially immature behavior. And that is a shame, for a close friendship died as a consequence.

As parents, we need to teach our children that good character entails not only doing the right thing up front, but also doing the right thing in the aftermath of wrong behavior, by oneself or by others. We need to teach our kids how to apologize when appropriate, but not when unnecessary or inappropriate.

We, as parents, need to teach our kids how to accept apologies as well as how to forgive others. Forgiveness is a true virtue. Most religious traditions highlight forgiveness, and there is research to demonstrate the therapeutic value of forgiveness, as well. (For more information on forgiveness research and its therapeutic power, go to www.forgiveness-institute.org or www.forgiving.org.)

Forgiveness ends negative feelings, heals psychic wounds, and repairs or builds positive relationships. So give your kids forgiveness; after all, forgiving is for giving character.

About the Author

Marvin W. Berkowitz is the inaugural Sanford N. McDonnell Endowed Professor of Character Education at the University of Missouri–St. Louis. Before arriving at UMSL, he was the inaugural Ambassador Holland H. Coors Professor of Character Development at the United States Air Force Academy. Previously he served as professor of psychology and director of the Center for Ethics Studies at Marquette University. He was also founder and associate director of the Center for Addiction and Behavioral Health Research in Milwaukee and adjunct professor of pediatrics at the Medical College of Wisconsin.

He was born in Queens, New York in 1950, attended public schools in Hewlett, New York, and earned a BA degree with honors in psychology from the State University of New York at Buffalo in 1972. He earned a Ph.D. in life-span developmental psychology at Wayne State University in 1977, after which he served as a research associate at the Center for Moral Development and Education at Harvard University for two years. He has taught at various institutions throughout the United States, Canada, and Europe. He has served as visiting professor at the Max-Planck-Institute for Human Development and Education in Berlin (1987-88), visiting scholar for the Gordon Cook Foundation in Scotland (1995), Ethicist-in-Residence at the University of South Florida (2002), and visiting scholar at Azusa Pacific University (2003).

His research interests are character education, moral development, adolescent development, and risk-taking. He is editor of *Moral education: Theory and application* (1985) and *Peer conflict and psychological growth (1985)*, and author of over 60 book chapters and journal articles. He serves as a board member of the Character Education Partnership and co-editor of the *Journal of Research in Character Education*. He has also served as an executive member of the American Bar Association's Interdisciplinary Committee to Promote the Best Interest of the Child and on the boards of the Jean Piaget Society and the Association for Moral Education. From 1990-1994, he was principal investigator of a four-year National Institute on Drug Abuse grant to study the relation of moral development to adolescent drug use. Dr. Berkowitz was named "Outstanding Young Educator of 1983" by the Milwaukee Jaycees, was cited as one of Milwaukee's "87 Most Interesting People" in *Milwaukee* magazine in 1987, and was invited to give the Henry Howe Chan Memorial Lecture at the Medical College of Wisconsin in 1992 and the first Great Midwest Conference Presidents' Lectureship in 1993. He was co-recipient of the 1994 University of Wisconsin–Milwaukee Community Partnership Award, was named "Best University Professor" in a "Best of Milwaukee '98" readers' poll of the *Shepherd's Express*, was inducted into the Hewlett-Woodmere Alumni Association Hall of Fame in 2001, and received the International Leadership Network "Applause Award" in 2004.

Dr. Berkowitz is author of a weekly newspaper column on parenting for character published in the *Topeka (KS) Capitol-Journal*. He is co-founder of ComedySportz, a nationally franchised improvisational comedy show, and has co-written a play *Chuck, Bob, and Louie*, which won best of show at the 1994 Milwaukee Festival of Ten Minute Plays. He has been married to Judith Gewanter Berkowitz for over 30 years and has one son, Daniel William Berkowitz, who was born in 1986.